The
Field
Experience

This series is dedicated in loving memory
to my parents, Daisy Lea and Weldon F. Appelt.
Through their love and devotion for me, I learned to
believe in myself and what I might be able to achieve in life.

The Field Experience

*Creating
Successful
Programs for
New Teachers*

Editor
Gloria Appelt Slick

CORWIN PRESS, INC.
A Sage Publications Company
Thousand Oaks, California

For information address:

 Corwin Press, Inc.
A Sage Publications Company
2455 Teller Road
Thousand Oaks, California 91320

SAGE Publications Ltd.
6 Bonhill Street
London EC2A 4PU
United Kingdom

SAGE Publications India Pvt. Ltd.
M-32 Market
Greater Kailash I
New Delhi 110 048 India

Printed in the United States of America

Library of Congress Cataloging-in-Publication Data

Main entry under title:

The field experience: creating successful programs for new teachers / edited by Gloria Appelt Slick.
    p. cm.
  Includes bibliographical references (p.) and index.
  ISBN 0-8039-6207-X (pbk.). — ISBN 0-8039-6206-1
  1. Student teaching—United States.   I. Slick, Gloria Appelt.
LB2157.U5F54   1995
370'.7'330973—dc20   95-7277

This book is printed on acid-free paper.

95 96 97 98 99 10 9 8 7 6 5 4 3 2 1

Corwin Project Editor: Susan McElroy

Contents

Foreword

Student teaching has long been considered the capstone of the teacher education program, and early field experiences have recently become a vital part of preparing teachers. Most teacher educators believe that field experiences should be integrated into the preparation of future teachers.

Because of this emphasis on field experiences, the position of director of field experiences has become even more important in teacher education. Where can field directors receive the information necessary to carry out the many and varied duties of the position? They tend to ask other field directors' advice. One of the most popular opportunities for field directors to share ideas is through membership in the National Field Directors' Forum, an affiliate with the Association of Teacher Educators.

The tenure of a field director is relatively short. The average tenure is between 3 and 5 years. Because of the turnover of field directors, there always seem to be new field directors literally craving information that will help them perform their duties.

Field directors recognize the need for some books that contain the information that both experienced and new field directors could use as a reference. A series of four books dealing with all aspects of field experiences, edited by Dr. Gloria Appelt Slick, fulfills the need. Directors around the nation welcome this series and I am proud to endorse this effort.

ELDEN R. BARRETT, PH.D.
FORMER PRESIDENT, NATIONAL FIELD DIRECTORS' FORUM

Foreword

Dear Educator:

As you read the material presented in this four-book series dealing with field experiences in teacher preparation programs, I hope you will bear in mind that this unique project is being brought to you from an institution whose history is rich in and founded upon teacher education. It has been through the leadership and dedication of such educators as Dr. Gloria Appelt Slick, editor of this series, that The University of Southern Mississippi, which was founded as Mississippi's normal school in 1910, continues to take a leadership role in the professional training of teachers.

I am proud to share with you this most recent endeavor of Dr. Slick, which focuses on the significance of field experiences in teacher preparation. Recent research by the Holmes Group, John Goodlad, and such accrediting agencies as the National Council for the Accreditation of Teacher Education has underscored the importance of the field experiences component of teacher education programs. This series of four books provides a review of state-of-the-art programs and practices in field experiences. The contributing authors represent prestigious teacher preparation programs from around the country. The information presented herein is solidly grounded in both research and practice. One of the main purposes of the four books is to provide practical guidelines for application of effective programs and practices in field experiences.

This is not the first time Dr. Slick has produced a national project that emphasizes field experiences. In 1993, through a national teleconference under the auspices of the Satellite Educational Resources Consortium, four interactive distance learning programs were broadcast to more than 200 sites nationally for the purpose of assisting student teachers, during their student teaching experiences, with their transition from university students to classroom teachers. From that series and the research involved to produce it evolved the current books, whose purpose reaches beyond student teachers and encompasses all persons, processes, and institutions affected by the field experiences component of teacher education. In both cases, Dr. Slick's overall goal has been to provide assistance and direction for all those involved in field experiences so that students of teacher education will be better prepared to meet the challenges of teaching the children of today and tomorrow.

Teacher education will always remain a major focus at The University of Southern Mississippi. We are committed to excellence in our teacher preparation programs and strive to develop the best of each of our students' abilities and expertise as future teachers. It is through such efforts as Dr. Slick's that we strive to meet that commitment.

Best wishes,

AUBREY K. LUCAS
PRESIDENT, THE UNIVERSITY OF SOUTHERN MISSISSIPPI

Preface

As a result of the Holmes Report, "A Nation at Risk," and other research, the wheels have been set in motion for a reflective and systemic change in the education profession. Both public schools and institutions of higher learning have had the national public spotlight on the quality of their educational outcomes and teacher preparation programs, respectively. Institutions of higher learning have adjusted their content and pedagogical requirements in their teacher education programs to try to meet the challenges of children who are products of the information age. Public schools have updated curricular offerings and made concerted efforts to tackle the innumerable problems relative to providing students and faculties with safe environments in which to teach and learn. Research by such educational leaders as Goodlad, Berliner, and Boyer emphasizes that the teachers of the future will need to participate early and continuously during their teacher preparation programs in the public school arena where they will eventually be employed. Nationwide, school districts and universities are forming collaborations that not only provide insight into the culture of the teaching profession for the novice teacher but also offer opportunities for veteran teachers to retool their skills as well as share their expertise with upcoming generations of new teachers. This bridge between the universities and the public schools, whether in the form of a professional development school, lab school, or local public school campus, provides, in essence, the pathway from student to teacher.

The program planning and management required to provide students in teacher preparation programs the opportunity to successfully cross the bridge from student to teacher are very complex. The bulk of the responsibility for providing students this successful crossing relies upon the collaborative success of teacher preparation programs and offices of educational field experiences. The director of the field experiences programs plays a principal role in managing the various persons and systems involved in the transitional passage of students to beginning teachers. It has been well documented by research that field experiences are the pivotal turning points in students' preparation for becoming teachers. During those experiences theory meets practice, and students discover whether they can teach or even want to teach. To date, for all persons and entities involved in this process, there is very little, if any, material available to assist in providing the best possible experiences for students aspiring to become exemplary teachers. The goal of this series of books is to provide field directors the information and practical guidance necessary to design and implement a successful field experience program that will provide individuals in teacher preparation programs a smooth transition from student to teacher.

Because the focus of these books is to provide information and practical guidance to all persons involved with field experiences in teacher preparation programs, it became a foregone conclusion that those persons contributing to this book should either be currently or have been recently affiliated with field experience programs. Most of the authors have actually been field experience directors, with the exception of those in specialty areas such as law and public school administration. In order for the book to be representative of a national view of the issues related to field experiences, much time and effort went into selecting persons representing a variety of types of institutions as well as geographic locations around the country. Attention has been given to the size of the teacher preparation programs offered at the various institutions that are represented in the books, with the intent to provide as many relevant views about field experience programs as possible in order to benefit cohorts everywhere. Institutions represented from the southeast include the states of Alabama,

Louisiana, Mississippi, Florida, and North Carolina; the northeast includes the states of New Jersey, New York, Pennsylvania, and Delaware; the midwestern states include Ohio, Kentucky, Illinois, Michigan, Iowa, Indiana, and Minnesota; the central states include Oklahoma and Texas; and the western states include Colorado, Arizona, Utah, and California.

Organization of the Books

In order to provide information and practical guidance for all the issues related to field experience programs, there are four books, each with a specific purpose. Book I, *The Field Experience: Creating Successful Programs for New Teachers*, provides information about the development and organization of field experience programs. It presents state-of-the-art field experience programs and explains what kinds of experiences should be provided to students. Other issues in Book I include the dilemma of the department chair who must provide a program that creates a balance between theory and practica, the dean's perspective of the significance of field experiences in teacher training, and the evaluation processes needed for field experiences programs. Book II, *Preparing New Teachers: Operating Successful Field Experience Programs*, presents practical ideas concerning the operation and function of the field experiences office and takes into account state department requirements relative to certification that also have an impact on field experience programs. Such issues as placement procedures as well as displacement procedures and the legal ramifications of both are discussed. The multifaceted responsibilities of the field director are presented, which brings to light the public relations that the director must handle, not only with the public schools but also across the various colleges and departments at a university/college. In addition, the purposes of field experiences handbooks are explained. Book III, *Making the Difference for Teachers: The Field Experience in Actual Practice*, addresses the needs and responsibilities of the persons involved in a typical field experience paradigm—the university student, public school personnel, and university personnel. Key issues such as effective communication and classroom management skills, effective mentoring, and adequate training of cooperating teachers are presented. Field experiences are explained from the student teacher's perspective, and the process of the student's assimilation of the culture of teaching is addressed. A major issue of concern is the preparation of cooperating teachers for the responsibility of supervising students. This is also dealt with in Book III. In addition, suggestions are made for ways to express appreciation to those who work so diligently supervising student teachers and other practicum students. Each of these issues has an impact on the university students' success during field experiences, and each topic is delivered in practical and applicable terms. Book IV, *Emerging Trends in Teacher Preparation: The Future of Field Experiences*, addresses areas of special interest affecting field experiences: (a) the promotion of reflective practices throughout all field experiences in teacher preparation programs; (b) the multicultural classroom environments education students will have to face; (c) the effective utilization of technology in field experience programs; (d) the awareness of legal ramifications of policies, or the lack of them, in field experience programs; (e) the development of leadership potential in pre-service teachers; (f) the support for the first year on the job; and (g) the special opportunities for student teaching field experiences abroad. A new look at the psychology of supervision is also presented along with a view of how the past can help us shape the future in field experiences. At the end of each book, there is a chapter titled "Bits and Pieces" that presents other issues that are critical to the overall success of field experience programs. Key points mentioned in each book are synthesized and analyzed. The information is presented in a somewhat encapsulated view along with additional points that may need mentioning.

The composite focus of all four books of the series is to provide the information and operational examples to assist others in offering strong, challenging, and viable field experiences programs throughout the country. The reader will find that each topic addressed in the books will place an emphasis on the practical application of the ideas and information presented. The series of books will provide readers not only with "food for thought" but also "food for action."

Acknowledgments

A massive project like this is only possible because of many wonderful people contributing their expertise, time, and energy into making it happen. From all over the country friends and colleagues worked diligently to contribute a special piece to one of the books. My sincere appreciation to my authors who patiently worked with me to complete this series.

Thanks also go to my office staff, Tina Holmes and Diane Ross, and to my university supervisors, Drs. Donna Garvey, Tammie Brown, Betsy Ward, and Ed Lundin, who kept the office running smoothly while I labored over "the books," as they came to be known in the office. Our office teamwork and philosophy of operation paid off during this project. Thanks go to my graduate assistants, Leslie Peebles and Amy Palughi, whose hard work during the initial stages of this project launched us with a good beginning. Most especially thanks go to Mrs. Lauree Mills Mooney, whose organizational and computer skills made it possible for the project to be pulled together in a timely manner. Mrs. Mooney's resourcefulness in overcoming obstacles and dedication toward completing the project were invaluable. In the final stages of proofing and indexing all the books, I want to thank Ms. Holly Henderson for her timely and critical assistance.

Thanks to special friends who encouraged me throughout the project: Dr. Margaret Smith, Dr. Kenneth Burrett, Dr. Chuck Jaquith, and Dr. Sandra Gupton.

The timely production and final completion of all four books could not have occurred without the kind and caring encouragement and guidance of the Corwin Press staff. My sincere thanks go to Alice Foster, Marlene Head, Wendy Appleby, Susan McElroy, and Lin Schonberger for their understanding and patience throughout this project.

A special thanks to my husband, Sam Slick, for his constant encouragement and support. Also, special thanks to my children, Andrew and Samantha, who patiently tiptoed around the house so Mom could think and compose in order to finish "the books."

About the Contributors

Linda Avila, currently a professor in the educational administration department of Texas A&M University—Corpus Christi, has supervised student teachers for 2 years and served on the team at Southwest Texas State University involved in its field-based teacher preparation program. She has additionally supervised administrative interns for 7 years and has more than 20 years of experience as a regular and special education teacher, principal, special education director, and assistant superintendent. She consults with several school districts on establishing teacher peer coaching models and implementing teacher study groups.

Kenneth Burrett is a professor in the school of education at Duquesne University and an associate in the center for character education, civic responsibility, and teaching. He also serves as a charter faculty member for Duquesne University's Interdisciplinary Doctoral Program for Education Leaders. A former elementary and secondary teacher and high school department chair, he has served as director of student teaching and associate dean at Duquesne. He received his bachelor of arts and master of science degrees from Canisius College and his Ed.D. from the State University of New York at Buffalo. He is active in Phi Delta Kappa, the Pennsylvania Association of Colleges and Teacher Educators (PAC-TE), and the Association for Teacher Educators (ATE). He was named Teacher Educator of the Year in 1989 by the Pennsylvania Unit of ATE. He serves on the board of Conservation Consultants, a nonprofit environmental organization; is past president of Western Pennsylvania Council for the Social Sciences; and serves on the board of PAC-TE and various committees of ATE. He has also secured numerous grants for inservicing veteran science teachers and encouraging career change individuals to enter teaching. This past year he coauthored a book chapter and *Phi Delta Kappa Fastback*, both concerned with integrated character education. He has also delivered numerous papers in the area of leadership theory and program design.

Charles R. Coble is dean of the School of Education, East Carolina University, where he has also served as professor of science education. He has written several articles in the field of science education and is the author of a major textbook in the field. At the present time he also serves as the chief researcher in a major national curriculum project in science, funded by the National Science Foundation.

Barbara Ann Coulibaly is director of student teachers and interns and is assistant professor in the Department of Curriculum and Instruction of the Benerd School of Education at University of the Pacific in Stockton, California. She has a broad range of experiences in teaching, consulting, and training in both the public and private sectors. For the past 10 years, she has provided training to early childhood programs in competency-based teacher preparation. Additionally, she consults in the areas of cultural diversity, conflict resolution, and intergroup relations. She holds an undergraduate degree in psychology from California State University at Los Angeles, a master's in education degree from Pepperdine University, and a Ph.D. in the psychology of education from Union Graduate School. She is currently working toward an Ed.D. in counseling psychology at University of the Pacific.

Pat Curtin has been in the field of education for more than 20 years as teacher, principal, and director of curriculum. During this time, she has worked extensively with university faculty and preservice teachers in the Southwest Texas Center for professional development and development for preservice and inservice educators at all levels. She holds B.S. and M.Ed. degrees from Southwest Texas State University.

Patricia D. Exner is coordinator of Teacher Education and Clinical Experiences for Louisiana State University's traditional, alternate certification, and Holmes teacher education programs. Drawing upon 17 years of experience as a secondary teacher, cooperating teacher, and university supervisor, she has been directly involved in the development of LSU's new Holmes teacher education programs, particularly in respect to the field experiences component.

Linda A. Fernandez received a B.A. from DePauw University, an M.S. from Indiana University, and an Ed.D. from Virginia Tech. She has 11 years experience in public school education in Iowa, Virginia, and Indiana, and 7 years experience in teacher education programs in Puerto Rico and Iowa. She is the director of Malcolm Price Laboratory School, University of Northern Iowa.

Allan A. Glatthorn is professor of education in the School of Education, East Carolina University. He served for 1 year as acting director of the University of Alaska Fairbanks School of Education and for 3 years as director of Teacher Education in the University of Pennsylvania Graduate School of Education. He is the author of numerous school textbooks and several professional books in the fields of curriculum and supervision.

Mildred E. Kersh is a professor of education and chair of the Department of Curriculum and Instruction at the University of Southern Mississippi. She has supervised student teachers as well as served as a clinical professor in field-based programs in the states of Washington and Mississippi. Her research interests lie in the areas of mathematics learning and teacher education, particularly models of teaching efficacy.

Rita M. King, Ed.D., is an assistant professor working with the Department of Educational Administration of the Benerd School of Education at the University of the Pacific, Stockton, California, and is one of two field experience supervisors in its educational administration credential program. She is president of the California Association for Professors of Educational Administration (1994-1995) and is a member of the California Collaborative for Educational Leadership, a partnership of several statewide organizations designed to integrate leadership preparation and development efforts in California. She is coauthor with Dr. Cheryl Fischer of *Authentic Assessment: A Guide to Implementation* and serves on the boards of the California Staff Development Council (CSDC) and the State of California Association for Teacher Education (SCATE). She earned her undergraduate, master's, and education specialist degrees from the University of Toledo (Ohio) and her doctorate in educational leadership from the University of San Diego (California).

Roger A. Kueter holds a B.A. from Loras College in Dubuque, Iowa, and an M.A. and an Ed.D. from Indiana University. He joined the staff of the University of Northern Iowa in 1970; has served as assistant to the dean and acting department head, Curriculum and Instruction; and presently is head of the Department of Teaching, administratively responsible for the divisions of the Malcolm Price Laboratory School and the Office of Student Field Experiences.

Kathlyn R. Oakland received her B.A. and M.A. from the University of Northern Iowa, Cedar Falls. After teaching speech and language arts in the Iowa public schools for 13 years, she returned to UNI as an instructor of speech and language at Malcolm Price Laboratory School. In 1991 she was the recipient of the Speech Communication Association's K-12 Speech Teacher of the Year Award. She is the pre-student teaching field experience coordinator in the teacher education program.

Susan E. Pullman is coordinator of student field experiences at Youngstown State University and is a member of the New Wilmington, Pennsylvania, Board of Education. She conducts workshops on "Writing the Final Evaluation," offered to cooperating teachers and presented at other universities, and has given national, state, and local presentations regarding practices in teacher education. She has served as an officer for the Ohio Association of Teacher Educators, National Field Directors' Forum, and the local chapter of Phi Delta Kappa. At present she is serving on YSU's International Studies Committee and the College of Education's

Long-Range Planning Committee. She holds an M.Ed. degree from Youngstown State University.

Virginia K. Resta is an assistant professor in the Department of Curriculum and Instruction at Southwest Texas State University, San Marcos. Her areas of expertise include teacher education in reading, language arts, and technology. She has been a teacher, clinical supervisor, and reading coordinator for a large urban school system. She has extensive experience in field-based pre-service and graduate-level teacher education programs and is currently coordinating a field-based professional development exchange program for first-year and experienced teachers.

Frank M. Ribich is a professor of education and chair of the Department of Educational Services in the School of Education at Duquesne University. He directs the student teaching program and coordinates the field experience program. He served basic education as a teacher of English, social studies, and Spanish and as a guidance counselor, supervisor of foreign languages, and administrator. He earned degrees from Duquesne University and the Pennsylvania State University and studied at the University of Pittsburgh as a postdoctoral student. His contributions to higher education are in program design at the undergraduate and graduate levels, portfolio development and assessment, and phenomenological validation procedures.

Mary J. Selke is an assistant professor of education and a doctoral faculty member at the University of Northern Iowa. Coordinator of a regional center for 2 years, she is currently coordinator at UNI's emergent professional development school. She has an established record of research and writing, with more than 35 publications and national presentations between 1992 and 1994, and is also active in professional organizations on the state and national levels.

Gloria Appelt Slick, a native of Houston, Texas, completed her doctoral work at the University of Houston in 1979. Her professional career in public school education has included classroom

teaching, supervision, the principalship, and assistant superinten-
dency for curriculum. In her current position as a faculty member
of the Department of Curriculum and Instruction and as Director
of Educational Field Experiences at The University of Southern
Mississippi in Hattiesburg, Mississippi, her past public school
experiences have provided her with significant insight into the
circumstances and needs of public schools for well-trained beginning teachers. During her tenure as Director of Field Experiences,
Dr. Slick has produced, in conjunction with Mississippi Educational Television, the first interactive distance learning program
to deal with the subject of field experiences, titled "From Student
to Teacher." These four programs were aired nationally in March
1993 and received the Mississippi Public Education Forum Award
for Excellence that same year. Dr. Slick is currently president of
the National Field Directors' Forum, affiliated with the Association
of Teacher Educators. She also serves on the editorial board of *The
Teacher Educator*. Her current research interests center on teacher
preparation programs and, in particular, the interface of field
experiences with those programs. Technological integration into
the field experience programs and field experiences abroad are also
high on her list of research and programmatic implementation.

Virginia Venglar is a third/fourth grade language arts teacher
and reading specialist at Bowie Elementary School, San Marcos,
Texas. She has served on the core team of classroom teachers
working with the Center for Professional Development and Technology at Southwest Texas State University for the past 2 years,
team-planning with university faculty and mentoring the field
experiences of teacher education students in her classroom.

Patrice Holden Werner is associate professor of reading education
in the Department of Curriculum and Instruction at Southwest
Texas State University in San Marcos, Texas. She has worked
extensively in field-based teacher education for 10 years and has
been a leader in developing and implementing the Southwest
Texas Center for professional development and technology, a collaborative entity that focuses on professional development for
preservice and in-service educators at all levels.

Introduction

GLORIA APPELT SLICK

This first book, *The Field Experience: Creating Successful Programs for New Teachers,* in a series of four presents a variety of field experiences program models and philosophies that drive the programs provided to preservice teachers during their undergraduate teacher preparation. Throughout the chapters in this book, even though they represent a variety of program models and philosophies, there emerge some common themes that are worth noting. First, each program appears to formulate a structure of passage that predetermines the path that undergraduate students must experience in order to assimilate the culture of teaching. Second, each emphatically expresses the belief that field experiences must be integrated thoroughly into the theoretical framework of teacher education programs. Third, it is only through this integration of efforts between the university faculty and clinical/field faculty that connections are made by the preservice teacher for practical application to the classroom. Unlike what Erdman (1983) indicated—" . . . it should be recognized that the quality of many early field experience programs is poor due to their inattention to the connectedness of theory and practice" (p. 27)—the programs outlined in this book stress the importance of this connection. They also exhibit sensitivity to the fact, as Clarken states, that participants in field experiences who do not have a knowledge base about the school as an institution, the student as a learner, and the teaching methods are not likely to benefit greatly from the experience (field experiences) regardless of how extensive the experiences might be (1993, p. 3). As expressed in this book, the fine balance between theory and practice is the ultimate goal of teacher education programs that value the need for both throughout their programs. In fact, the National Council for the Accreditation of Teacher Education emphasizes "that teacher education programs are to make certain that clinical and field-based experiences are designed to prepare students to work effectively in specific education roles"(1987, p. 41). The NCATE's definitions of clinical experiences and field-based experiences indicate the significance that accrediting body places on practica experiences:

> *Clinical Experiences:* Clinical experiences are those that are characterized by careful planning, stipulated goals, required activities, projected performance levels, and evaluation of growth. Included are micro teaching clinics, participation experiences, skill clinics, developing case studies of individual students, curriculum development clinics, and use of instructional technology or computers. These are conducted both as school based and campus based experiences. Activities not meeting the criteria for clinical experiences might include general observations, voluntary community service, orientation visits, teacher aiding, and periodic visitations to educational settings. (p. 54)

> *Field-Based Experiences:* Field-based experiences are conducted at a school site, a school administration center, a school clinic, or community agency. These experiences might include classroom observations, tutoring, assisting school administrators or teachers, participation in school and community-wide activities, student teaching, and internships. Planning is shared by the professional education unit and the appropriate agency. (p. 55)

Other themes that emerge from the representative chapters and programs mentioned herein are (a) the need for close working relationships between the university faculty and the public school agents, (b) the need for committees composed of persons representative of interested parties to serve in an advisory capacity to the field experiences programs, (c) the need for well-articulated field experience programs, and (d) the need for valuative criteria for the students being assessed in the programs as well as the need for valuative criteria for overall program effectiveness.

For field experience programs to be effective, they must be generated from a strong philosophic base that values the significant role they play in the overall teacher education program. It is through the professional field experiences that concepts, generalizations, or theories that are emphasized in the professional sequence are evaluated with respect to their relevance and usefulness in the real world (Clarken, 1993, p. 5). Far too often preservice teachers have few opportunities in their undergraduate programs to practice their teaching competencies. They spend most of their undergraduate time acquiring further knowledge of their subject matter and yet, in study after study, preservice teachers indicate that the most valuable and helpful experience they had during their entire teacher preparation program was their student teaching. It stands to reason that if this final experience provides the most significant training component for neophyte teachers, other field experiences that can serve as connectors with the real world should also be an integral part of teacher preparation programs. In Smith and Sagan's (1975) taxonomy of field experiences there are five parts: (a) orientation, (b) conceptualization, (c) learning and commitment, (d) assumption, and (e) evaluation. This taxonomy is based on the following view:

> The education of the professional is a longitudinal process of theory and practice, rather than a procedure of five semesters of professional theory capped by student teaching. If we are to prepare professionals who can properly utilize the behavioral science concepts of pedagogical theory in making instructional decisions, who can analyze

educational needs, who can select and innovate appropriate materials, and who can benefit from self-analysis and
evaluation, we must establish a new school-college parity
in the preparation of teachers. It is essential that more
theory, not less, be included in the professional sequence
and that these concepts be clinically and analytically experienced through public school field experiences and
situational analysis. (Smith & Sagan, 1975, p. 90)

Therefore, as the chapters in this book indicate, careful consideration of close collaboration of universities and public schools
is a must if preservice teachers are to receive optimum opportunities for relevant field experiences that are grounded in sound
pedagogical theory as well as a solid knowledge base.

References

Clarken, R. H. (1993, April). *Clinical and field-based experiences to
    prepare teachers for wholistic practice.* Paper presented at the
    annual meeting of the American Educational Research Asso-
    ciation, Atlanta, GA.
Erdman, J. (1983). Assessing the purposes of early field experience
    programs. *Journal of Teacher Education, 34*(4), 27-31.
National Council for the Accreditation of Teacher Education
    (NCATE). (1987). *NCATE standards, procedures, and policies for
    the accreditation of professional education units.* Washington, DC:
    Author.
Smith, C., & Sagan, E. (1975, January). A taxonomy for planning
    field experiences. *Peabody Journal of Education, 58,* 89-96.

Creating State-of-the-Art Field Experiences

The Professional Development School

MARY J. SELKE
ROGER A. KUETER

Nearly a decade ago, *A Nation Prepared: Teachers for the 21st Century* (Carnegie Forum, 1986) and *Tomorrow's Teachers* (Holmes Group, 1986) served as catalysts for reform that challenged teacher preparation institutions to close the gap between the ivory tower world of pedagogical theory and the practical reality of contemporary classrooms by establishing more intensely collaborative partnerships with pK-12 schools. Collaborative partnerships between pK-12 schools and institutions of higher education (IHEs) have since been identified as essential to a quality teacher preparation program (Association of Teacher Educators, 1991; Clemson,

1990; Griffin, 1986; Renaissance Group, 1989). Studies have documented resulting benefits of school-university partnerships for pK-12 students (Wise, Darling-Hammond, Berry, Berliner, Haller, Praskac, & Schlechty, 1987), beginning teachers (Holmes Group, 1990), in-service practitioners (Selke & Kueter, 1994), and university faculty (Chambers & Olmstead, 1991).

In spring 1987, the University of Northern Iowa (UNI) responded to the challenge of restructuring teacher education with a reconceptualization of the relationship between the College of Education (COE), pK-12 schools, and other forces that have an impact on teacher education. The resulting relationship between schools and the university is expressed in the Venn diagram, *A Teacher Education Program at the Intersection of Institutional Structures*, designed by COE Dean Thomas Switzer in April 1991 (see Figure 1.1). Teacher education is the central element; the parallel sets of arrows emphasize the interactive nature of the linkage connecting the university and the world of practice, resulting in a model that involves many forces in the reciprocal enactment of systemic change.

Theoretical Basis of the UNI Model

Since the mid-1980s, many models of school-university partnerships have evolved that go beyond simply placing preservice students in schools for practicum experiences. One example of such partnerships is the teaching center model, which involves clustering preservice teachers in several school districts and assigning resident professors to those centers to coordinate placement, observation, and evaluation of preservice teachers (McIntyre, 1979). Benefits of teaching centers include (a) the skill, knowledge, and access to campus resources provided by resident university faculty (Gardner, 1979); (b) easier communication of teacher education policies and practices to field site personnel; (c) more efficient communication of cooperating teachers' concerns back to campuses; and (d) the facilitation of theory into practice derived from placing preservice programs in field-based sites (McIntyre, 1994). The commitment of resident professors who guide the

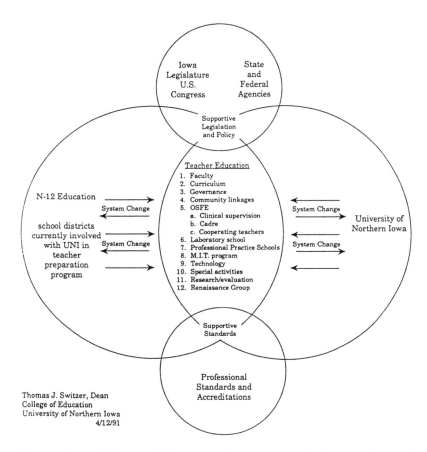

Figure 1.1. A Teacher Education Program at the Intersection of Institutional Structures
SOURCE: University of Northern Iowa. Reprinted with permission.

activities of teaching centers is often the pivotal factor in teaching center effectiveness (Quisenberry, McIntyre, & Byrd, 1990).

Another example of school-university partnerships is the professional development school (PDS) model, originally proposed to encourage new structures designed to meet developmental growth needs of teachers, administrators, and college faculty (Holmes Group, 1986, 1990; Stallings & Kowalski, 1990). The common mission of professional development schools is to unite school-based practitioners and IHE faculty, "in partnerships that improve teaching and learning on the part of their respective students" (Holmes Group, 1986, p. 56). This mission is enacted and benefits to both parties are derived through four core components: (a) mutual deliberation on problems associated with student learning in order to generate possible solutions, (b) shared teaching in IHE and school settings, (c) collaborative research on the problems of educational practice, and (d) cooperative supervision of prospective educators (Holmes Group, 1986). Although all components are not necessarily present in any given PDS partnership (Winitzky, Stoddart, & O'Keefe, 1992) the common mission and core components form the basis of PDS partnerships.

Overview of the UNI Model

The school-university partnership in place at UNI blends elements of the teaching center and the professional development school. As in teaching centers, UNI students are assigned to regional centers under the guidance of a professor coordinator. As in professional development schools, professor coordinators collaborate with teaching associates cadre members and clinical supervisors to solve problems associated with center-specific delivery of the UNI student teaching curriculum, share some teaching responsibilities, conduct collaborative research on the problems of educational practice related to preservice practica, and supervise prospective educators.

The mission of the UNI model focuses upon engaging cadre members and clinical supervisors in the collaborative supervision of prospective educators. Clinical supervisors perform the same duties as professor coordinators in regard to the direct supervision of student teachers. Cadre members assist through the formal or informal mentoring of student teachers. Cadre members at each center were initially selected by the regional professor coordinator but are now chosen by existing members in collaboration with their regional coordinator.

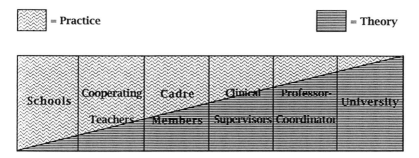

Figure 1.2. Theory/Practice Continuum

The UNI model spans the "people gap" between college professors and school-based practitioners by establishing a smooth continuum that features varying levels of formalized involvement in schools and the university for educators based in both educational cultures (see Figure 1.2). The resulting model is unique in that it combines the best elements of the teaching center and the professional development school. It provides a statewide network of regional professional development centers, with outreach centers currently being established in national and international settings, that involve school-based practitioners more closely and more directly in the preservice preparation of educators.

The Teaching Associates Cadre/Clinical Supervisor Model was implemented by restructuring a statewide system of field sites into 10 regional student teaching centers based in urban areas throughout the state. Clinical supervisors, jointly selected and employed by the university and a school system within the respective regional centers, assist professor-coordinators with coordination of the center and supervision of practicum experiences.

Teaching associates cadre members in each center are master teachers and experienced cooperating teachers who form professional partnerships with professors and clinical supervisors in the centers to provide linkages between schools and the university. From its inception, the design of the model called for each of the newly aligned regional student teaching centers to establish its own center-specific school-university partnership identity, guided by cadre members. This constructivist approach generated some initial confusion but resulted in a strong, comprehensive implementation of the model that meets site-specific needs in each center.

The original model provided for 5 volunteer cadre members in each regional center, each to be paid a stipend of $500 per year by the university. At present, regional center profiles indicate changes in the structure of many cadres that address center-specific needs. Some cadres have grown from 5 members to almost 20, allowing for a cadre member in each field-site building and resulting in creative usage of stipend monies. Although some cadre members continue to receive the amount as an annual salary, others use it to offset the expenses of professional development opportunities, such as presentations at national teacher education conferences. Still other cadre members pool their stipends for cadre activities carried out in the centers.

Participants in each center are engaged in the facilitation of teaching and learning on the part of their respective students. On campus, cadre members have spoken in methods classes, assisted with curricular review, and participated on campus panels and projects. Clinical supervisors provide a readily available link to university resources or personnel through their bimonthly overnight trips to campus for departmental meetings. Although cadre members in the regional centers are more isolated from campus and from each other, UNI supplements Internet capabilities via the biannual cadre conference, for which cadre members around the state come to the UNI campus for 2 days of interaction, reflection, and meetings with methods faculty.

In the regional centers, cadre members and clinical supervisors may lead student teaching seminars or orient new cooperating teachers. Clinical supervisors or cadre members may also assist with exit interviews, recruit cooperating teachers, facilitate communication between student teachers and cooperating teachers or building administrators, and help students from outside the center find housing for the duration of their student-teaching experience. Some cadres take a more extended role by facilitating the placement and supervision of pre-student teaching practicum students, especially those who will be working in cadre members' schools.

Collaborative Implementation:
Keys to Making It Work

Effectiveness of a collaborative, reciprocal model of teacher education depends upon the quality of connection between schools and campus. A crucial element in the UNI school-university connection is a team of professor coordinators who are committed to field-based practitioner involvement and the fostering of dynamic school-university partnerships. Coordinators must either be personally well connected on campus and in the field center or receive assistance until such contacts are established on both ends. Without commitment to the partnership concept and the ability to facilitate the necessary connections, a critical mass of expertise and interest may be assembled in the field centers or on campus without any interaction occurring.

Another crucial element in a school-university connection is the ability of both parties to accept that the partnership will be (a) *formalized* in a partnership agreement that clearly identifies expectations of both parties to the best of their ability upon initiation, with the agreement to revisit the document at regular intervals to allow for changes, and (b) *actively* collaborative, including resources of time and money essential to productive involvement of personnel. This is especially true of the school districts that host regional centers by providing such necessities as office space, seminar meeting rooms, and readily available placements for student teachers. Willingness of school districts to go beyond passively opening their schools to student teachers is essential.

The most readily apparent symbol of this willingness is the joint selection and appointment of one or more clinical supervisors. Districts remain responsible for providing clinical supervisors with benefit packages identical to those of full-time teachers. Districts also provide release time and substitute teachers to cover bimonthly campus overnight meetings for clinical supervisors and, in many cases, assistance with expenses incurred in connection with professional conferences.

At the foundation of the partnership is active commitment from the campus. The University of Northern Iowa has been a teacher education institution since it was established as the Iowa

State Normal School, and teacher education remains central to the university's mission. Education majors currently predominate, as they have historically, composing almost one third of the student population.

If active support from the campus and potential centers is assured, a university wishing to build a network of professional development centers must prepare for the responsibility that comes with the initiative of developing such a partnership: managing and assessing the partnership effort. Tasks related to management will deal mostly with facilitating communication between involved parties. This responsibility can be as simple as providing distance communication systems such as faxes, car phones, E-mail and Internet capability, or fiber-optic cable access. It can also be as complicated as convincing reluctant campus-based faculty members that field practitioners, though they may not have read the latest research journals, have working knowledge of today's classrooms that is invaluable to teacher educators who are preparing university students to teach in tomorrow's schools.

Once the partnership is in place, assessment helps keep the relationship vital and focused on improving the quality of teacher education. At UNI, mail surveys of cadre members are conducted at regular intervals. Work of clinical supervisors is reviewed annually. Clinical supervisors and coordinators keep in touch with school administrators to glean their perspective on the partnership's effectiveness. In addition, clinical supervisors and cadre members maintain close contact with center coordinators, who update university personnel on the effectiveness of the model as it operates within each center.

The Teaching Associates Cadre/Clinical Supervisor Model currently in place at the University of Northern Iowa has been a driving force behind a statewide network of professional development centers that combines elements of teaching centers and professional development schools. Collaborative interaction between educators involved in this schools-university partnership provides student teachers with state-of-the-art clinical preparation, which is essential for success in today's schools. Principle #3 of the Renaissance Group states that "those who practice in the schools are partners in conceptualizing, planning, developing, and delivering teacher education programs" (Renaissance Group, 1989). UNI's Teaching Associates Cadre/Clinical Supervisor Model provides a comprehensive network of professional development centers that sets a new standard for practitioner involvement in the teacher education process.

References

Association of Teacher Educators. (1991). *Restructuring the education of teachers: Report of the commission on the education of teachers into the 21st century.* Reston, VA: Author.

Carnegie Forum on Education and the Economy. (1986). *A nation prepared: Teachers for the 21st century.* New York: Author.

Chambers, M., & Olmstead, B. (1991). Teacher corps and portal schools. *Portal Schools, 1*(1), 2-8.

Clemson, S. (1990). Four models of collaborative teacher education: A comparison of success factors and maturation. *Action in Teacher Education, 12*(2), 31-37.

Gardner, W. (1979). Deans' perspective of support for teachers in the beginning years. In K. Howey & R. Bents (Eds.), *Toward meeting the needs of the beginning teacher* (pp. 95-110). Minneapolis: Midwest Teacher Corps Network and University of Minnesota/St. Paul Schools Teacher Corps Project.

Griffin, G. (1986). Clinical teacher education. In J. Hoffman & S. Edwards (Eds.), *Reality and reform in clinical teacher education* (pp. 1-23). New York: Random House.

Holmes Group. (1986). *Tomorrow's teachers: A report of the Holmes group.* East Lansing, MI: Author.

Holmes Group. (1990). *Tomorrow's schools: Principles for the design of professional development schools.* East Lansing, MI: Author.

McIntyre, J. (1979). Integrating theory and practice via the teaching center. *Contemporary Education, 50*(3), 146-149.

McIntyre, J. (1994). Partnerships and collaboration in the contexts of schools and teacher education programs. In M. O'Hair & S. Odell (Eds.), *Partnerships in education: Teacher education yearbook II* (pp. 1-10). New York: Harcourt Brace.

Quisenberry, N., McIntyre, J., & Byrd, D. (1990). Collaboration and reflectivity: Cornerstones of a teacher education program. In H. Schwartz (Ed.), *Collaboration: Building common agendas.* Washington, DC: American Association of Colleges for Teacher Education.

Renaissance Group. (1989). *Teachers for the new world: A statement of principles.* Cedar Falls: University of Northern Iowa, Renaissance Group.

Selke, M., & Kueter, R. (1994, February). *School/university partnerships and the UNI teaching associates cadre model: Professional benefits to preK-12 educators.* Paper presented at the meeting of the American Association of Colleges for Teacher Education, Chicago. (Eric Document Reproduction Service No. ED 369 728)

Stallings, J., & Kowalski, T. (1990). Research on professional development schools. In W. R. Houston (Ed.), *Handbook of research on teacher education* (pp. 251-266). New York: Macmillan.

Winitzky, N., Stoddart, T., & O'Keefe, P. (1992). Great expectations: Emergent professional development schools. *Journal of Teacher Education, 43*(1), 3-18.

Wise, A., Darling-Hammond, L., Berry, B., Berliner, D., Haller, E., Praskac, A., & Schlechty, P. (1987). *Effective teacher selection: From recruitment to retention* (R-3462-NFE/CSTP). Santa Monica, CA: RAND.

Articulating
Field Experience Programs

KATHLYN R. OAKLAND
LINDA A. FERNANDEZ
ROGER A. KUETER

Rapid change in American society, corresponding to the growing acknowledgment of a global society, has resulted in increased focus on the preparation of people to assume their places as contributing and thinking citizens in an uncertain future. Preparation of future citizens inevitably and rightfully falls largely to our education system. The national recognition for the need to improve the system of education is represented by the Goals 2000 document.

Among a series of goals focusing on United States education, Goals 2000 challenges teacher educators to improve access to programs for continued professional improvement through "establishing goals for students and schools, encouraging states and school districts to adopt rigorous standards for their education system, and improving the quality of teaching in K-12 schools" (Earley, 1994, p. 7). This holds multiple implications for higher education: improvement of preservice teacher education programs; increased availability and quality of continuing education; and the necessity of forming substantive partnerships with departments of education, schools, and practicing educators. Higher education must prepare students who can demonstrate the knowledge, skills, and attitudes to enter the education profession and to grow as educators to meet the changes and challenges of an uncertain future.

The University of Northern Iowa (UNI) Teacher Education Program is predicated on beliefs that are consistent with the direction of the goals described by Goals 2000. We believe that teacher education is the shared responsibility of university faculty, practitioners, and other related professionals. We believe that the initial preparation of teachers is best integrated throughout the students' university experience. We believe that the education of teachers incorporates extensive and sequenced field experiences. These beliefs provide the basis for the structure and content of the Teacher Education Program. The UNI Teacher Education Program requires successful completion of a comprehensive program of studies consisting of three components: (a) a general education requirement; (b) study of the subject content area(s) and grade levels; and (c) the professional education program, which includes a sequence of courses and experiences in professional studies and teaching methodology.

Teacher education students develop a knowledge of human development, learning, and sociocultural factors as the basis for pedagogical decision making. They develop skills of observation, reflection, decision making, and the ability to transform content knowledge into the knowledge necessary for future professional responsibilities. In these ways, students become teachers who are responsible, reflective decision makers in a global society.

The commitment to outcomes required for success is clearly demonstrated by the Field Experience Program, that portion of the Teacher Education Program that precedes student teaching.

Throughout the content area/grade level and professional education components, students observe and participate in an extensive number of teaching and learning experiences in different classroom settings.

The goal of the Field Experience Program is to guide teacher education students through progressive stages of the pre-student teaching period by engaging them in numerous and varied experiences.

Teacher education students are able to make informed decisions concerning their careers. They participate in experiences that will facilitate their determination of grade level and subject area preparation. They gain valuable experience with pupils of varying social and cultural backgrounds.

Students are required to present themselves as preservice professionals, participating in instructional and noninstructional activities both within and outside the immediate classroom assignment. They interact with other students, teachers, and administrators in educational settings.

This chapter will describe the field experiences that are an integral part of the UNI Teacher Education Program. The sequence, rationale, expectations, evaluation methods, and student comments for each level of field experience are included. Because of its complexity, the structure of the Field Experience Program can be bewildering to students, university faculty, cooperating teachers, and administrators. In an effort to ease this problem, a baseball analogy has been adopted: The common vocabulary and understanding of first base, second base, and so forth alleviates the potential for confusion within and among diverse audiences. So, let's play ball!

First Base

First Base or Level I is Exploring Teaching, a corequisite to the core course, Dynamics of Human Development, and is the first of a graduated series of field-based experiences. This field experience is an introduction to the world of teaching. It provides students with an opportunity to learn by doing through working in a classroom situation. The overall goal of this experience is to help students begin thinking of themselves as professionals in the school.

While on First Base, students become familiar with the roles, responsibilities, and professional relationships of teachers and the multiple dimensions of child development. Students observe skills and abilities common to all teachers and teaching, not specific content areas or grade levels. It is through this observation and limited participation at First Base that students understand more realistically the demands of teaching and whether their abilities and interests are consistent with professional demands.

First Base requires 30 contact hours, consisting of 3 hours per week for 10 weeks in a single classroom located in a local school. These students are beginners in teacher education and are in the classroom for minimal time each week, and this experience focuses on the qualities necessary to be an effective teacher.

Students are assigned to a school and are supervised by university faculty. Taking into consideration personal preferences of grade or content area, students select their classroom placements from a list of volunteer teachers in schools.

Several orientations are provided by faculty on topics of professionalism, attendance, ethics, responsibilities, and portfolios. Assessment and attendance are recorded by the cooperating teacher in consultation with the student and faculty.

First Base classroom experiences provide students with the opportunity to observe examples of the patterns and variations of development discussed in the corequisite course, Dynamics of Human Development.

Comments collected from student evaluations following their First Base experience are insightful. Samples include:

"It confirmed to me that I am in the right field."

"I was able to interact with students for the first time."

"I had the opportunity to apply what I had learned."

Second Base

Second Base or Level II Field Experience is Teacher as a Change Agent, a corequisite to Nature and Conditions of Learning. Second Base requires a minimum of 25 hours. Each semester consists of three 4-week sessions, contributing to the intensity of the experience and flexibility in scheduling. Faculty members in the Department of Teaching and the Department of Educational Psychology and Foundations coordinate the placement and supervision processes.

The goals for the Second Base Field Experience center around three elements of instruction. The first area is classroom management: Students observe and practice strategies of preventive and interventive management to optimize student learning. The second area is motivation, in which students explore intrinsic and extrinsic motivation while practicing the methods demonstrated by teachers. The teaching/learning process is the third goal area. Students identify and observe strategies used in effective teaching as they plan, develop, and deliver instruction. They also evaluate lessons from the perspective of behavioral and cognitive learning principles.

Students demonstrate an understanding of the concepts and principles taught by citing the ways in which the concepts and principles are applied by enlisting and sustaining pupil motivation to learn; citing measures teachers use to manage classroom activities; and teaching at least one lesson to a small group, a class, or an individual.

The students demonstrate a responsible and ethical commitment to teaching by seeking a variety of ways to assist the teacher. Through conferencing with the cooperating teacher, students acquire greater confidence by practicing and reflecting on the professional significance of the principles of learning, motivation, and classroom management.

The role of the cooperating teacher is paramount at this base. All Second Base students are placed at Malcolm Price Laboratory School, a division of the Department of Teaching. Laboratory School faculty serve as the coordinating teachers for this field experience.

Laboratory School faculty and Department of Educational Psychology and Foundations faculty collaborate to supervise the Second Base experience. Laboratory School faculty demonstrate in their classrooms and via the telecommunication system. They process experiences with students, recommend materials and resources, plan lessons with the students, evaluate students' teaching performances, and advise students concerning educational issues and trends.

Evaluation is an ongoing process and includes attendance; initiative; poise; interpersonal relations with pupils, teachers, and parents; and performance in class activities and written work. Assessment is recorded on a pass/no credit basis.

Students review their evaluations with their teachers. Conferences are conducted for developmental and evaluation purposes. The following comments were written by students during their Second Base experiences:

> "At first I seemed overwhelmed and as an outsider but, in the few weeks I have been with these students, I began to feel more comfortable and they began to ask me questions and (for) advice. This makes me feel like my education has been worthwhile and I am more knowledgeable about areas I am not familiar with."

> "In working one-on-one with a student in this short amount of time I have seen her go from an unsuccessful learning situation and having low motivation to being very successful and motivated to succeed."

> "I learned the difference between lecturing a lesson and actually teaching and adjusting to the students while giving the lesson."

Shortstop

Occasionally a student is not ready to advance to the next base or level. Following conferences involving the student, cooperating teacher, supervising faculty, and Pre-Student Teaching Field Experience Coordinator, the student may be placed at "shortstop." This remediation step allows a student to repeat or expand on an experience in order to achieve the required outcomes prior to advancing to the next level. Cooperatively, a plan is developed defining the amount of time, specific experiences, activities, products, and evaluation criteria. Through this team effort, the student will strengthen areas in need of remediation. The student does not advance until Second Base is completed satisfactorily.

Third Base

Level III or Third Base consists of the Professional Semester, during which students complete teaching methods courses in the individual colleges of the university. Each methods course requires a field experience consistent with the course content, best practice methods, and state certification requirements.

An example of one of the Third Base field experiences is the "On the Road" experience required in conjunction with the elementary/ middle school Classroom Management course. All students leave campus and participate all day, every day, for a full week in a classroom located in 1 of the 13 UNI student teaching centers. Student Teaching Coordinators at each center facilitate the placement of "On the Road" students. This field experience allows students to participate in the continuity, and unpredictability, of instruction over the course of a full week. Students experience the complexity of the teacher's role and responsibilities, gain insights into individual student differences over a period of time, and plan and conduct instruction with the cooperating teacher. A key aspect of this experience is involvement in the entire act of teaching: planning, facilitating learning, and assessment.

Overall the preferred experiences associated with the methods courses occur when students are involved in ongoing activities. The Third Base Field Experience requires that students assume a measure of responsibility for an entire class. Throughout the experience, students assess personal strengths and weaknesses under the guidance of the cooperating teacher.

Comments recorded by students following their Third Base experience include the following:

"I was exposed to a variety of cultures, experiences, students and strategies."

"I learned how to think on my feet and adjust the lesson so it was appropriate for the learners."

"I worked with a diverse group of children in a lower income area, so I learned a lot from this experience."

Home Plate

Student Teaching or Home Plate provides students the opportunity to experience in depth the full role and meaning of teaching. Student Teaching is one semester and emphasizes analysis of teaching and learning, organization of instructional content, adaptation of techniques to organization and content, the logical process of teaching, and principles of independent self-evaluation.

This pattern of experiences includes developing classroom teaching competencies and skills, evaluating pupil progress, participating in school life outside the classroom, and utilizing school and community resources in the instructional program.

The Student Teaching program places a high priority on developing a preservice teacher's ability to become a reflective practitioner. Time is committed to learning, experimentation, critical analysis, and practice of the skills necessary to reflect effectively and plan accordingly.

It is the intent of this experience to create awareness in students of the range of professional practices. The program prepares students to adapt curriculum, methods, and behaviors to improve instruction. Students are able to demonstrate readiness to assume the roles and responsibilities of a professional practitioner independently.

Evaluation remains an ongoing process. Factors considered in the Student Teaching evaluation include demonstration of teaching skills in context, reflective journals, concurrent seminar participation and performance, action research, and conferences.

Comments made by students following their Student Teaching experience include:

> "Student teaching offered many, diverse, real teaching experiences."

> "It prepared me for my own classroom."

> "I had plenty of opportunity to teach and to deal with the 100+ other facets of teaching."

Career

Will the players be recruited by the National League? The American League? Or will players be in a "league of their own"? When students leave campus their coaches are confident that each player is prepared as a professional educator. As reflective practitioners they are capable of self-direction and self-correction. They know how to seek out additional coaching and how to work as part of a team. They graduate into the university rather than from it. Teacher Education (to the tune of "Take Me Out to the Ballgame"):

> Take students out to the classrooms,
> Take students out to the schools,
> Give them more than red ink and books:
> We're sure they have the right tools!

Reference

Earley, P. M. (1994, April). *Goals 2000: Educate America Act implications for teacher educators*. Washington, DC: American Association of Colleges for Teacher Education.

Leadership for
Effective Student Teaching

ALLAN A. GLATTHORN
CHARLES R. COBLE

T his chapter challenges two prevailing and contrary beliefs. The first is that the dean of the school of education can singlehandedly provide leadership for the student teaching program; the second is that the activities of the dean have no consequence for the quality of that program. (Note that throughout this chapter the term *school of education* is used as a convenient means of designating schools, colleges, and departments of education.) Our central theses hold that team leadership is needed here and that such leadership can make a profound difference in the quality of the student teaching experience.

An Argument for Team Leadership

The current literature on elementary and secondary school reform gives significant attention to the importance of team leadership, especially emphasizing the value of faculty involvement in decision making (see, e.g., Sergiovanni, 1994). However, there is scant reference in the literature on the need for team leadership in higher education. Perhaps this dearth of research results from the assumption that the traditional emphasis on the power of university faculty is sufficient to produce effective teamwork. As Clark and Guba (1980) noted, although the predominant governance pattern in higher education is a collegial one, no one is specifically trained in the skills needed for collegial governance.

Our experience suggests clearly that the dean should organize, support, and use a team-leadership structure, especially for the needs of the student teaching program. Although the specific nature and function of that team will, of course, vary with the institutional context, an analysis of the literature and our own experience would suggest that the program would operate effectively with the following organizational structures: the student teaching assembly, a comprehensive body composed of all students and professionals involved in student teaching; a council of teacher education, a representative leadership group; and a school-site leadership team, a school-based group designed to solve pressing problems.

If these groups are to be effective, they must be seen as active and influential bodies that act in a manner that operationalizes the following principles:

- The university and the school are equal partners in the development of high-quality professionals.
- The expertise of effective classroom teachers, school principals, and university faculty are all valued; they can learn from one another in a climate of openness and inquiry.
- The autonomy of each constituent institution is respected; neither attempts to prescribe for the other.

- Consensus is desired and achieved through open deliberation.
- Student concerns are important and should be recognized and responded to; student power should be legitimized and operationalized within the limits of school and university policies.

Such structures for team leadership in no way diminish the authority of the dean and the need for the dean to exercise strong leadership. As Dill (1980) noted, the dean is the major force in universities for innovation and constructive change. In understanding the critical role of the dean as a leader in a collegial organization, the leadership functions identified by Edmundson (1991) seem most useful: identifying needed changes and encouraging development of a vision, communicating clearly within and outside the university, obtaining needed resources, ensuring continuity of resources and personnel, supporting limitations on enrollment on the basis of the program's capacity to provide high-quality field experiences, promoting ongoing renewal of teacher education, committing to continuing improvement, supporting the development of an organizational unit that has as its central mission the preparation of educators, and delegating responsibility to a faculty and staff who possess the requisite knowledge and experience and who demonstrate a commitment to the preparation of educators.

Exercising Leadership Across Campus

As several experts have noted, the school of education is held generally in low regard by other schools and departments within the university (see, e.g., Clifford & Guthrie, 1988; Goodlad, 1990). Rather than simply bemoaning this sad state or reacting defensively to criticism, the leadership team needs to take several specific actions in three categories: *quality improvement, collaborative problem solving,* and *image enhancement.*

Quality improvement is a reminder that, when it comes to enhancing the images and status of the school of education and the student teaching program, there is no real substitute for improving quality. If the school and its student teaching program are perceived across campus as vital organizations seeking and achieving improved quality, then the image can be significantly improved. A case in point is the situation at East Carolina University: When its highly successful Model Clinical Teaching Program received first place recognition at the 1994 annual conference of the Association of Teacher Education, the attendant publicity in community and campus newspapers made a perceptible difference in the way faculty from other departments and schools viewed the teacher education and student teaching programs.

Collaborative problem solving involves school of education faculty and faculty from other schools in the university in cooperative efforts with local school systems. As has been pointed out in several reports, such collaborations can succeed only when all participants are seen as equal partners, when there is a commitment on the part of leaders to ongoing and sustained collaboration, when there is shared decision making, and when needed resources are provided in timely fashion (see, e.g., Bercik, 1991; Grobe, 1993). When such collaborations are successful, faculty involved develop an increased respect for one another. At the University of Alaska-Fairbanks, for example, the active collaboration of the School of Education science educators with faculty from science departments in projects serving regional schools had a positive influence on both groups of university faculty. As Sidney Stephens, a prime mover of the project, noted, the education faculty gained an appreciation of the dynamic nature of scientific knowledge and of scientific inquiry as a powerful means of asking and answering questions; science faculty learned about new teaching strategies and current developments in learning theory and research. Stephens concludes, "This cross fertilization has enriched the dialogue about the goals and methods of science education" (S. Stephens, personal communication, June 1, 1994).

Image enhancement involves undertaking direct and systematic strategies to create a more positive image of the school and its student teaching program. If the quality is improved and collaborations are supported, then related strategies to improve the image are likely to succeed. On the other hand, as stated earlier, attempts to enhance the image of the school of education, when there is neither a commitment to improvement nor genuine collaboration, are futile and, in the long run, counterproductive. The following strategies can be successful when built upon a foundation of substance.

- Holding high visibility conferences on campus dealing with current educational issues, inviting university administrators and faculty from other schools to play an active role in planning and conducting the conference.
- Sponsoring informal faculty seminars on campus that bring together faculty from all units within the university to examine current educational issues.
- Publicizing collaborative efforts with local schools, focusing on the teamwork involved in the preservice education of teachers.
- Taking an active and leading role in helping other schools and departments improve the quality of teaching.
- Giving special attention to improving the image of the school of education among chief university administrators.

This last strategy is especially important. The president and the provost (and their analogues with other titles) can influence campus opinion about the school of education and can deliver special resources. Despite the anti-administration stance of some faculty, university faculty in general value a dean who has a good working relationship with university administrators and who can use that influence in securing scarce resources.

The dean is therefore in a unique position to use such strategies as the following in influencing other higher-level university administrators. Because such officers are generally aware of the present concern for school reform, the dean should keep them informed about the efforts of faculty and administrators in the school of education to work collaboratively with schools in reform efforts. Calling attention to specific faculty and program accomplishments is also useful and appropriate, as long as this is done selectively. Occasionally deans make the mistake of highlighting accomplishments that would seem insignificant to the chief administrators. Finally, significantly involving them in major programs sponsored by the school of education is also helpful. Such involvement should be more than delivering a perfunctory welcome; from time to time these chief officers should be invited to participate in an open discussion with faculty and public school educators on current issues in higher education.

All the above strategies are concerned with improving the status of the school of education, not simply focusing on the student teaching program. Although that should be given appropriate attention in such plans, the argument here is that enhancing the status of the entire school among university faculty and administrators will yield benefits to the student teaching program over time.

Exercising Leadership
Within the School of Education

The leadership exercised in the school of education should focus more specifically on the student teaching program. This area needs special attention, because the student teaching program and faculty are often held in low regard by the rest of the faculty, especially by graduate faculty in research-oriented universities (see the review by Corrigan & Haberman, 1990).

The first task of leadership is to ensure organizational cohesiveness so that student teaching is seen as an integral part of a comprehensive preservice program, rather than as a low-status appendage. Such cohesiveness has three related aspects. *Structural cohesiveness* is achieved through the team leadership structures explained above, as they provide for substantial representation and involvement of the student teaching faculty, the rest of the professional faculty, and faculty from other schools in the university. *Interpersonal cohesiveness* results when the dean and the director of student teaching provide specific opportunities for student teaching faculty and other school of education faculty to interact around common concerns. If, for example, the state develops a new curriculum framework for science, the dean would be wise to convene one or more sessions in which faculties from the science department, the teacher education program, and the student teaching program would examine the implications of the framework for teacher education. *Program cohesiveness* is accomplished when the teacher education faculty ensure that general education, professional education, and the student teaching experience are closely aligned. Students in one teacher education program with which we are acquainted suffered the consequences of misalignment when the university supervisor required them to develop a science unit emphasizing student inquiry although they had received no instruction in linking the principles of unit development and the concepts of constructivism, so important in science education. As Guyton and McIntyre (1990) note, such problems of discontinuity are unfortunately too common in teacher preparation programs.

The second task is for the leadership team to work with the student teaching faculty to develop and articulate both a vision of student teaching and a set of clear expectations that will guide program development and implementation. It should be noted here that Fullan (1993) reminds change agents that the best vision emerges from practice; we adapt this principle by recommending that the team articulate the vision early on and then revisit it from time to time. We have found that the following process works effectively in developing the initial draft.

- Assemble all those to be involved, organizing them into groups of five or six.
- Present each group with the opening phrase: "We have a dream of a student teaching program that is . . . "
- Ask participants to work individually at first. Each one without discussion begins by identifying five key adjectives that best capture the essence of the vision. For example, someone might write the adjective *reflective*. That individ-

ual then writes one sentence explaining the adjective, as in this example:

Reflective: The students are guided to reflect before practice, during practice, and after practice.

- In the small groups, the participants share their work and agree on the five key adjectives and elaborating sentences that best represent their thinking.
- The results from each small group are then synthesized into one collective vision.

The leadership team then uses this vision to articulate clearly its expectations for the student teaching experience. Such expectations should be reasonably high—challenging, but attainable. Here is one set we have used with faculty.

We hold the following expectations for the student teaching program.

1. Students will enter the program with a solid knowledge of the principles and practices of effective teaching and learning and with an in-depth mastery of pedagogical content knowledge.
2. The student teaching experience will be closely integrated with and be a natural extension of preservice on-campus course work.
3. The student teaching experience will provide for increasing autonomy for the student teacher.
4. The university supervisor, the cooperating teacher, and the student teacher will work collaboratively to foster the growth of all involved.
5. The university supervisor, the cooperating teacher, and the student teacher will be sensitive to emerging problems and will use effective problem-solving strategies in a climate of openness and cooperation.
6. All faculty involved with student teaching will model a high standard of professionalism and expertise.

7. Cooperating teachers and university supervisors will be carefully selected and provided with effective training in the supervision of student teachers.

8. Student teachers experiencing difficulties will be provided with appropriate and timely remediation.

9. No student will be recommended for certification who has not demonstrated mastery of the basic skills of effective teaching and an internalization of the principles of professionalism.

The next task of leadership within the school of education is to enhance the status and improve the performance of university supervisors. In too many instances untrained graduate assistants and retired teachers are given the crucial task of supervising student teachers, with these accompanying low-status attributes: low salaries, lack of an office, heavy supervisory loads, and marginal professional status. In a time of downsizing and budget cutting, it may be unrealistic to make radical changes here in relation to loads, salaries, and faculty status. It should also be noted that, as Lamb and Montague (1982) discovered, graduate assistants can be effective supervisors when they are provided with effective training. However, there are changes that can be made without requiring excessive budget support.

- Select university supervisors with the same care that tenure-track faculty are selected, evaluate their performance, and terminate ineffective supervisors.

- Develop and implement a comprehensive training program on effective supervision and evaluation of student teachers; as noted below, such training should also involve the cooperating teachers.

- Clearly define the respective roles of the university supervisor and the cooperating teacher. (See below for a fuller discussion of this issue.)

- Provide a central office where all university supervisors can meet to discuss common problems, have access to professional resources, view videotapes of teaching, and confer with student teachers when the latter are on campus.

- Increase the number of full-time supervisors and place them on tenure-track lines, reducing the number of part-time and adjunct faculty.
- Recognize the special contributions of university supervisors through merited praise in faculty meetings and school publications.
- Provide for celebrations (such as end-of-year dinners and awards ceremonies) of the accomplishments of university supervisors.

Next, the dean should ensure that the student teaching experience is carefully evaluated as a total program, not only to improve that program but also to provide evaluative data for the entire teacher education program. In this sense the culminating student teaching experience is seen as a valid measure of program effectiveness.

Finally the leadership team needs to give special attention to the hidden curriculum of the school of education. Defined variously by several experts in the field, the term *hidden curriculum* is used here to mean the implicit messages transmitted to the student through the structures, relationships, policies, and practices of the school. As Ginsburg and Clift (1990) indicate, the hidden curriculum of too many preservice teacher education programs is replete with negative messages about teaching. Consider, for example, what students would learn from these aspects of the hidden curriculum of the student teaching program.

- The student teaching office is one of the smallest in the school.
- University supervisors are the lowest paid members of the faculty.
- The supervision of student teachers is not adequately reflected in computations of faculty load.
- The dean rarely appears at meetings of the supervisors or at end-of-year celebrations.

- The accomplishments of the student teaching program are rarely publicized.
- Cooperating teachers are neither recognized nor adequately rewarded.
- The most experienced teachers are reluctant to work with student teachers.
- Student teachers have no input in such decisions as the site, the cooperating teacher, the nature of their assignments, and their evaluation.
- Supervisors and cooperating teachers dominate the debriefing conferences with student teachers.

Such negative messages must be countered by the work of the leadership team as it analyzes the existing hidden curriculum of the student teaching program and makes changes that will convey a more positive image.

Exercising Leadership With the Cooperating Schools

The final and perhaps most important domain for the exercise of leadership is in developing significant collaborations with the cooperating schools. Other chapters in this book delineate a variety of models for achieving such collaboration. The research and our own experience suggest that the following principles of practice are more critical than the specific features of particular models.

First, roles are clearly defined. The research is both conclusive and persuasive that serious difficulties develop in the student/cooperating teacher/university supervisor triad when there is role ambiguity (see the review by Guyton & McIntyre, 1990). In clarifying roles, the leadership team should give serious attention to those models (described in this book and elsewhere) that stress the importance of the cooperating teacher as the primary supervisor. As Glickman and Bey (1990) point out in their review, the cooperating teacher's role has been cited as influential, important, and essential. Because some experts in the field of supervision recommend making a clear distinction between *development* and *evaluation* and assigning these tasks to different individuals, the team should seriously consider defining the role of the cooperating teacher as providing development (with no official responsibility for evaluation) and that of the university supervisor as providing evaluation (see Glatthorn, 1990, for the arguments for such differentiation). In this model, the cooperating teacher is thus perceived as an experienced peer mentor who provides evaluation input to the university supervisor only when the student teacher requests it.

Second, the student teaching experience replicates as fully as possible the experience of the first-year teacher. The student teaching experience lasts a full school year, follows the school calendar, and makes it possible for the student teacher to engage fully in the critical opening and closing periods of the school year. The student teacher participates in all the professional experiences provided the certified staff; the only major difference is that the student teacher begins the year under the close guidance of the cooperating teacher, moving systematically to full autonomy.

Third, the cooperating teachers play an active role in the campus program, working cooperatively with university faculty to assist with methods courses, demonstrating their expertise as needed, identifying and solving problems associated with the student teaching experience, and providing individual coaching to student teachers needing remediation.

Fourth, the practicum is supported and extended by reflective practice seminars. These are regularly scheduled sessions involving all student teachers, cooperating teachers, and university supervisors. Their objective is to transcend the limitations of practice by raising the level of reflection and discourse. As the research indicates, student teaching runs the risk of crystallizing for the student traditional concepts of teaching and learning (see, e.g., the review by Guyton & McIntyre, 1990). The reflective seminars counter such an effect. The participants analyze the nature of effective teaching by viewing videotapes of both experts and novices, reflect about their own teaching in peer-mediated viewing of tapes, identify and share solutions to problems encountered in their student teaching, and discuss current issues of teaching and learning. As McCaleb (1984) determined in a follow-up study of seminar participants, involvement in such seminars was associated with more effective performance in the first year of teaching.

Next, the three members of the triad participate actively in training programs that improve supervisory skills, increase awareness of new approaches to teaching and learning, and foster a cohesive professionalism. Glatthorn's experience in working with the Fairbanks (Alaska) schools indicates that such programs foster collaboration, enhance the image of the school of education, help cooperating teachers and university supervisors become more effective as supervisors, and increase the student's knowledge of the purposes and practices of supervision (see his 1994 monograph).

A Concluding Note

Deans of schools of education carry many responsibilities and respond to several constituents. However, we firmly believe that facilitating team leadership for the student teaching program should be a high priority among all those responsibilities.

References

Bercik, J. T. (1991, November). *School based/university collaborative effort: A preservice model.* Paper presented at the annual conference of the National Council of States on Inservice Education, Houston.

Clark, D., & Guba, E. (1980). Schools, colleges, and departments of education: Demographic and contextual features. In D. Griffiths & D. McCarty (Eds.), *The dilemma of the deanship* (pp. 67-90). Danville, IL: Interstate.

Clifford, G., & Guthrie, J. W. (1988). *Ed school: A brief for professional education.* Chicago: University of Chicago Press.

Corrigan, D. C., & Haberman, M. (1990). The context of teacher education. In W. R. Houston (Ed.), *Handbook of research on teacher education* (pp. 195-211). New York: Macmillan.

Dill, W. (1980). The deanship: An unstable craft. In D. Griffiths & D. McCarty (Eds.), *The dilemma of the deanship* (pp. 261-284). Danville, IL: Interstate.

Edmundson, P. J. (1991). *What college and university leaders can do to help change teacher education.* Washington, DC: American Association of Colleges of Teacher Education.

Fullan, M. (1993). Innovation, reform, and restructuring strategies. In G. Cawelti (Ed.), *Challenges and achievements of American education* (pp. 116-133). Alexandria, VA: Association for Supervision and Curriculum Development.

Ginsburg, M. B., & Clift, R. T. (1990). The hidden curriculum of preservice teacher education. In W. R. Houston (Ed.), *Handbook of research on teacher education* (pp. 450-465). New York: Macmillan.

Glatthorn, A. A. (1990). *Supervisory leadership.* New York: Harper-Collins.

Glatthorn, A. A. (1994). *Fostering collaboration through problem solving seminars.* Greenville, NC: East Carolina University.

Glickman, C. D., & Bey, T. M. (1990). Supervision. In W. R. Houston (Ed.), *Handbook of research on teacher education* (pp. 549-566). New York: Macmillan.

Goodlad, J. I. (1990). *Teachers for our nation's schools.* San Francisco: Jossey-Bass.

Grobe, T. (1993). *Synthesis of existing knowledge and practice in the field of educational partnerships.* Washington, DC: U.S. Department of Education.

Guyton, E., & McIntyre, D. J. (1990). Student teaching and school experiences. In W. R. Houston (Ed.), *Handbook of research on teacher education* (pp. 514-534). New York: Macmillan.

Lamb, C. E., & Montague, E. J. (1982, February). *Variables pertaining to the perceived effectiveness of university student teaching supervisors.* Paper presented at the annual meeting of the Southwest Educational Research Association, Austin, TX. (ERIC Document Reproduction Service No. ED 212 613)

McCaleb, J. L. (1984). *An investigation of on-the-job performance of first-year teachers who are graduates from the University of Maryland, from December 1982 to August, 1983.* College Park: University of Maryland, Department of Curriculum and Instruction.

Sergiovanni, T. J. (1994). *Building community in schools.* San Francisco: Jossey-Bass.

4

Providing
Meaningful Field Experiences

FRANK M. RIBICH

For meaningful experiences to occur in the field experience component of the teacher education program, the program structure and the processes within the structure must be meaningful to the participants from the onset. To increase the probabilities for meaningful experiences for preservice teacher candidates, a conceptual framework of the program that illustrates the organizational structure and the processes valued in the program must be communicated. A structure/process approach provides a critical advance organizer—the basis for students to plan for field experiences and to anchor and integrate the experiences with prior knowledge.

This chapter will provide the reader with an example of meaningful structure and meaningful process that was designed and implemented at a major urban university. As a prerequisite to that piece, however, I will examine briefly field experiences in teacher education in general and will discuss contextual demographics that will influence the design and implementation of the field experience component of any teacher education program.

Field experiences for students in teacher education programs became a common feature of those programs in the 1980s. There is ample literature that addresses a wide range of topics on the subject. The probability is that all institutions that house teacher education programs incorporate some form of field experiences because it is politically, as well as professionally, correct to do so. Field experiences are simply accepted as important and worthwhile in the professional development of teachers.

State departments of education have established requirements for field experiences. The Association of Teacher Educators (1986) has developed guidelines for the field experience component of teacher education programs, and the National Council for the Accreditation of Teacher Education (1992) has established standards for field experiences. There is, indeed, agreement that field experiences are a necessary and valuable part of preservice education.

There are two powerful arguments that support field experiences in teacher education programs, particularly in the freshman and sophomore years (Ribich, Agostino, Barone, & Birch, 1982). The first argument suggests that the person of the teacher candidate is central to the educative process. In the initial stages of the teacher education program, student growth in self-awareness, social effectiveness, decision making, and exploration are most effectively enhanced by a close working relationship of field experiences to classroom activities at the college or university. The integration of fieldwork and class work at this level should promote opportunities for students to observe in classrooms, reflect, examine themselves psychologically in relationship to becoming teachers, and interact with professionals and students in diverse settings.

The second argument is that the fusion of theory and practice and the fusion of reflection and action require a strong connection between the college or university program and the real world of the schools in the community. The fact is that the schools of the community are the natural allies of the colleges and universities in preservice education.

In line with the characteristics of field experiences proposed in state department of education mandates, professional association guidelines, and accrediting body standards, the arguments presented above would suggest that field experiences should:

- Be initiated as soon as possible in the preservice program
- Be an integral part of the whole curriculum
- Be carefully planned and linked to course work
- Be sequential and developmental
- Provide opportunities for students to experience a wide range of settings and learners who represent a variety of socioeconomic backgrounds

Although there is general agreement about the characteristics of a solid field component of the teacher education program, there is less agreement about what "field experiences" means, what the scope and sequence of the field experiences should be, who should supervise the field experiences, what the nature of the supervision should be, what the source of the field experiences should be, in what settings students should have field experiences, and when field experiences should be scheduled. Decisions around these issues will depend upon the philosophical and psychological aspects that govern a particular teacher education program, as well as the presence or absence of some very pragmatic resource and demographic variables.

The teacher education program should meet the requirements of the characteristics stated above and control those variables as best possible, but in all fairness to those who coordinate those programs, there are many variables over which the college or university coordinator has little or no control. For example, the college or university class schedule may preempt any desirable time frames for the field experiences and secondary majors in certain cognate areas may be impacted by scheduling restrictions; the number of schools in the surrounding communities available as field sites and the number of cooperating teachers available present other areas of concern. Additionally, transportation, the availability of physical space in the schools, the nature and the quantity of learning materials available to the students and faculty, and the school district bell schedule all influence the quantity and quality of the field experiences.

Other elements that affect the efficacy of the field experiences are (a) the size of the cohort, (b) the size of the department or school of education, (c) the goals and objectives of the teacher education program, (d) the fiscal resources of the unit, and (e) the personnel resources of the unit. These elements, coupled with the demographics of the school site or agency, will affect the quantity and quality of opportunities at the site, the quantity and quality of supervision and feedback, and the time spent at field sites.

As the range of field experiences expands from the freshman year to the induction year, the coordination of activities will become more complex. Because it is extremely difficult for all preservice students to have an identical experience, common kinds of experiences are more possible. Even when students attend the same school site for the field experience, the influence of the cooperating teacher, the learners in a particular class, and the physical and social milieus will affect the intended outcomes. Nevertheless, my experience with students in the field indicates strongly that the field experience is critically important to growth and development as a teacher, even a bad experience contributes.

To this point, I have outlined generally accepted characteristics of quality field experience programs. I have also addressed the notion that field experience programs are likely to be different between schools or departments of education because of philosophical orientation and/or demographic variables that will have an impact on the program.

To provide a foundational framework for the concept of meaningful experience, I will borrow quite liberally from the work of Getzels and Guba (1957) on administrative and organization theory and from foundations steeped in phenomenological and humanistic psychology. I will illustrate operationally that meaningful experience is a product of the integration of organizational and subjective phenomena in the context of a field experience program.

According to Getzels and Guba, any organization, such as the school, the program, or the curriculum, represents a social system that involves two major classes of phenomena:

1. The *nomothetic phenomena* are represented by roles and expectations of the school, the program, or the curriculum. These phenomena are designed to meet the goals of the organization. In the case of education, these goals will be influenced by state standards and by accreditation body requirements.
2. The *idiographic phenomena* are represented by the personalities and need dispositions of the individuals involved in the enterprise, that is, the students and the faculty.

Professional and social behavior in the enterprise, therefore, is composed of the interactions of the two phenomena. An equilibrium of the two phenomena produces satisfaction, productive relationships, and productive outcomes, which are essential to the continuation of participation of both the person and the organization. My personal experience suggests that the development of meaningful experiences in the positive sense of the words requires field experiences that are nomothetically and idiographically compatible and comprehensible. Nomothetically, field experiences will be meaningful if students are provided with a conceptual framework of the proposed field experiences from the freshman year through student teaching. The description and illustration of the framework give students not only an advance organizer from which to frame their own experiences but also a structural tool to process the experience. Idiographically, field experiences will be meaningful if students have opportunities for reflective practices that merge historical analysis and oral and written description. As a result, the form, shape, and substance of experience can be understood more clearly.

In 1978 several of my colleagues and I utilized these notions by blending a looming competency-based orientation in teacher education with an internal humanistic philosophy. A program was designed that nomothetically accepted the notion of "becoming" as a central and pervasive theme, a theme that emphasized the lifelong search for the meaning of self. We reasoned that the search would promote dialogue with self and others and would expand one's perceptual field and allow for creativity and experimentation, learning how to learn, and commitment to teaching and learning.

Four major organizational domains were structured around the central theme of "becoming." The domains served the curricular functions of sequence, integration through subsumption, and exploration around the theme for the year. The domain for the freshman year was "becoming a person"; the sophomore year focused on "becoming a student of education"; the junior year emphasized "becoming an educational theorist"; and the senior year, particularly student teaching, centered on "becoming a practitioner." In the vertical structure, the higher domains subsumed the lower domains. Each domain integrated team-taught course work and field experiences. The purpose of all of the activities in the domains was to have the student "become a teacher," a person who could confidently respond to "Who am I as a person?" "Who am I as a teacher?" "Will students learn from me as a person?" and "Will students learn what I intend to teach?"

Students participated in a field experience every semester from the freshman year through student teaching. Assignments for the experiences were designed by the core curriculum faculty and were intimately tied to the domain in which students were enrolled. Students observed teaching and tutored middle school learners in a structured setting in the freshman year. The sophomore experience was devoted to small group instruction, tutoring, facilitative activities, and work as a teacher aide. Large group instruction was the target activity in the junior year. Student teaching was the capstone experience in the senior year. All of these experiences provided ample opportunities for students to experience current practice, analyze methods, cooperate, collaborate, develop professional qualities, and the like.

The core curriculum consisted of 27 credit hours, which focused on the development of 18 generic competencies. The underlying assumptions of the curriculum were:

1. There is a common body of knowledge that all teachers need.
2. There are multiple means of assessing student performance.

3. There is a vital need to integrate classroom activity with field experiences.
4. A constructivist approach to generating meaning is valid and viable in teacher education.
5. The curriculum should reflect a synthesis of humanistic and professional dimensions.
6. Curricular experiences will be meaningful if students are given an advance organizer that conceptualizes the structure and processes of the curriculum.

Special features of the core curriculum were:

1. A competency-based orientation grounded in phenomenology and humanistic psychology.
2. Extensive and integrated field experiences beginning in the first semester of matriculation.
3. Team teaching and team assessment of student progress.
4. Reflective practice and subjective explication processes delivered in a staffing format each semester.
5. Horizontal continuity and vertical articulation of content topics and processes.

Idiographically, we believed in multiple opportunities for acculturation and socialization, and freedom to interpret phenomena in an open forum. These notions were grounded in phenomenology, which, in the broadest sense, refers to the lived quality of the inner experience of individuals, how they perceive the external world, and how they react to those perceptions in concrete situations (Georgi, 1975). That notion suggests that the interpretation of phenomena is fundamentally subjective. Core faculty, therefore, attempted to directly influence and strengthen student reflectivity, self-awareness, and knowledge and understanding of actions performed and the rules by which actions were taken. Happily, we discovered that students were able to increase communicative competence through our encouragement to express their perceptions and, as a result, were able to make quite abstract knowledge quite practical. The ultimate goal was to educate students to process perception and to validate competence through the explication of their involvement in field experiences. In that sense, the student could become the preactive, interactive, and postactive constructor of experience.

Two qualitative construction processes were designed to elicit description: (a) a log relating to the field experience and (b) a portfolio or "staffing" document, which was designed to support claims relating to the competencies of the program. Both required reflection and self-reference and were meant to measure meaning directly, without measuring in the strictest sense of the word. The students communicated their meanings in both personal and cognitive terms that demonstrated their awareness of and their involvement in their experiences. Speaking and writing about one's self became a well-informed and well-grounded validation process.

"Staffing" was the occasion at which the students presented the reflections, explications, and claims to competence based upon their work and experiences during each semester. The staffing consisted of three basic steps: (a) compilation of data to support and demonstrate competency development, (b) preparation of written testimony to competence to be presented orally to peers and faculty, and (c) feedback from peers and faculty and recommendations for future development.

Written logs of field experiences were a significant part of reflective practice and historical analysis. Logs provided opportunities for students to describe events, to cognitively and affectively react to those events, and to test personal meaning regarding beliefs, values, and commitments. The cumulative effect of these self-reflective processes was the development of communication skills, which revealed evidence of students' confidence in presentation, initiative, and skills in time management.

Opportunities for meaningful field experiences will be enhanced if, in the nomothetic sense, students are educated regarding the conceptual framework of the program and the gamut of proposed field experiences from the freshman year through student teaching. Within that framework, students will learn to construct meaning as they interact idiographically with nomothetic phenomena. As students share their meanings with others, they will learn that they own what they mean.

References

Association of Teacher Educators. (1986). *Guidelines for professional experiences in teacher education.* Reston, VA: Author.

Georgi, A. (1975). Convergence and divergence of qualitative and quantitative method in psychology. In A. Georgi, C. Fischer, & E. Murray (Eds.), *Duquesne studies in phenomenological psychology: Vol. II.* Pittsburgh: Duquesne University Press.

Getzels, J. W., & Guba, E. G. (1957). Social behavior and the administrative process. *The School Review, 65,* 423-441.

National Council for the Accreditation of Teacher Education. (1992). *Standards, procedures, and policies for the accreditation of professional education units.* Washington, DC: Author.

Ribich, F., Agostino, R., Barone, W., & Birch, J. (1982). A case for early field experiences. *Journal of Professional Studies, 8*(1), 16-22.

Recommended Reading

Georgi, A. (1970). *Psychology as a human science: A phenomenologically based approach.* New York: Harper & Row.

Getzels, J. W. (1958). Administration as a social process. In A. W. Halpin (Ed.), *Administrative theory in education.* Chicago: University of Chicago, Midwest Administration Center.

❖ 5 ❖

Feedback Measures in Field Experience Programs

PATRICE HOLDEN WERNER
LINDA AVILA
VIRGINIA K. RESTA
VIRGINIA VENGLAR
PAT CURTIN

As preservice teachers develop their skills in teacher training programs, they are bombarded with knowledge and experiences from which they must construct the complex schema that eventually constitute teaching "expertise" (Berliner, 1986; Livingston & Borko, 1989). Field experiences provide authentic contexts in which preservice teachers gain this complex teaching knowledge. However, research by Zeichner (1980) and others indicates that field experiences alone are inadequate and can, in fact, be "miseducative" rather than positive learning experiences. Feedback measures are one vehicle for improving the quality of field experiences and guiding the professional development of preservice teachers.

Feedback consists of information about a learner's performance that helps the learner grow. In field experience settings, feedback is the process of facilitating interns' learning from practice experiences in classrooms. Feedback responses from various sources, such as university faculty, clinical faculty, or peers, help interns analyze what happens in their field experience and, more important, generalize to future situations.

The Southwest Texas Center for Professional Development and Technology (SWT-CPDT) has developed a preservice teacher education model focusing on intensive field experiences prior to student teaching. Professional education courses are "blocked" and team-taught in area public schools with an emphasis on integrating course content and field experience. Interns experience the holistic nature of teaching while constructing a knowledge base, gaining practical expertise, and becoming reflective teachers. Feedback, a critical component in this effort, provides the bridge between knowledge, thinking, and experience. This chapter describes the comprehensive system of field experience feedback developed in this model.

Purposes of Feedback

The SWT-CPDT feedback measures are used for a variety of purposes depending on the context and needs of interns. These purposes range from very specific and directive to more general, self-initiated, and reflective and include (ranging from more directive to more reflective):

- teaching specific skills
- connecting specific skills/concepts to experience
- reinforcing positive teaching behavior
- correcting misconceptions, misapplications
- guiding and/or encouraging reflection

- encouraging self-assessment and self-reward

The ultimate goal is for interns to become self-assessing and reflective professionals; however, sometimes more directive feedback is necessary. It is important to continually assess the intern's developmental needs while determining the appropriate purpose, type, and level of feedback.

Types of Feedback

The formative and nonevaluative feedback measures described below are used throughout the field experience to guide and support learning. Nonevaluative feedback is critical in creating a nonthreatening environment that empowers interns to make decisions, express their opinions, and learn from their inevitable mistakes. For interns to become more self-assessing, they must have ample opportunity for self-reflection that provides internal feedback. Interns in the SWT-CPDT have primary responsibility for providing their own feedback, enabling them to become independent, reflective practitioners. External feedback from university faculty, clinical faculty, peers, or others complements, guides, and supports the intern's self-reflection.

Intern Self-Reflection

Interns reflect in writing on their experiences, questions, and learning in public school classrooms using *daily reflection forms* with the following four stems:

- Observations/Experiences
  (Briefly describe what you saw and did)
- Opinions/Reactions/Questions
  (How it went and why . . .)
- How I Felt/What I Learned . . .
- I Wonder . . .

Similar to a journal, these daily reflections encourage interns to immediately process their daily learning. University faculty read these reflections and respond with comments, encouragement, praise, and questions to further challenge interns' thinking.

A highly important self-reflection activity is a *written self-evaluation* following each teaching episode. Interns respond to the following stems for each section of their lessons:

- How Did It Go?
- How Do I Know?
- Why Did It Go the Way It Did?
- If I Were Teaching This Lesson Tomorrow, What Would I Do Differently? Why?

Using these stems, interns are able to analyze and judge the effectiveness of their lessons, as demonstrated in these responses:

"Using the overhead with a worksheet for guided practice that closely resembled the independent practice worksheet worked well. Students knew exactly what to expect during independent practice."

"If I were teaching this lesson tomorrow, I would wait to give directions to the class after materials have been distributed, and I would have an extension activity available for students who complete their work before others."

"The students were very attentive and interested during the reading of *Pecos Bill*, but I think they might have understood better if they had worked on a cause/effect web together as a class before doing it in cooperative groups."

"My task directions were pretty specific. I wrote down a lot of what I said and went into quite a lot of detail. This helped me to organize what I was to do. I think one of the reasons my lesson was successful was because of the time I spent here."

Some interns, however, experience difficulty with substantive reflection and make shallow comments, and others blame the students when lessons do not work:

> "I heard some kids fussing at each other to work on the fable. They were aware of the goal. The best students made sure they finished the fable. . . . Only a few students attained the social goals [for cooperative learning]. They can't do it."

Remarks such as these provide opportunities for university faculty to respond and shape interns' thinking. In response to the last example, the university faculty commented: "Perhaps these children *can* do it, but have not had the guidance and opportunity to learn. Had they worked in cooperative groups before you tried this activity? Do you think if you were able to concentrate on these social group skills over time that you would see a difference?"

A valuable form of feedback requires interns to *teach some of their lessons twice* to different groups of students. This requirement gives self-reflections more purpose, as interns immediately put their thoughts into action. They no longer reflect hypothetically (*"If* I were teaching this again tomorrow . . . "), but authentically ("I *am* teaching this again tomorrow. How can I make this go better?"). Consequently, interns consider the quality of their original judgments and determine their abilities to assess a situation and adjust. This strategy has proven to be a powerful learning experience when interns correct what they see as teaching mistakes. Knowing that they can learn from their mistakes increases their efficacy and reinforces the importance of self-reflection.

A *self-report checklist*, a simple feedback form listing required and optional field experience activities, ensures that interns complete many different instructional and managerial activities and ensures that clinical faculty provide adequate opportunities for interns to learn common routines and procedures, such as taking roll and lunch count. This list is developed collaboratively with teachers who determine appropriate activities for interns to complete in their classrooms.

Clinical Faculty Feedback Measures

Clinical faculty act as both models and mentors for interns in their classrooms. Because clinical faculty are "real teachers," their feedback is highly valued by interns and may profoundly affect intern self-confidence in planning and managing instruction. While providing feedback to interns, clinical faculty must continually consider appropriate performance expectations.

Because clinical faculty observe the intern in day-to-day interactions with children, much of their feedback takes the form of *spontaneous praise and suggestions* for handling situations arising in the classroom.

Clinical faculty also *supervise the planning of formal lesson presentations* by interns, ensuring each lesson's benefit to their students, determining the curriculum area to be taught, and providing guidance on the appropriateness of the planned lesson content and activities for that particular class. Interns are encouraged to try out ideas from their university classes, but clinical faculty retain the responsibility for evaluating lesson flow and preventing at the planning stage any obvious problem areas. A delicate balance exists between allowing interns freedom to create and make choices, and ensuring that experiences are successful and enhance intern confidence.

When interns present formally planned lessons, clinical faculty observe student reactions, make *informal observation notes* on strengths and weaknesses in instructional behaviors, and provide suggestions for future variations in the lesson:

> "I like the way you responded to the students as you did when Micah pointed out that 'playful' and 'playing' were too close. You asked for alternatives, praising his analysis."

> "When you stood beside the student who was speaking, he spoke very quietly. Try standing across the room from the speaker so the speaker will speak loud enough for the whole class to hear."

This feedback demonstrates for interns the effective teaching practice of evaluating lessons based on student response and adjusting lessons to meet student needs. These informal notes are discussed with each intern as soon as possible after the lesson is presented. The *conference* is initiated by the question, "What do you feel were the strengths and weaknesses in your lesson?" Discussion then focuses on areas that most concerned the intern.

Communication between clinical and university faculty is essential. Clinical faculty needs to be informed of the instructional strategies and philosophies being emphasized in university classes so that all parties are aware of any serious differences between what is being taught at the university and what is being practiced in the classroom. For example, if interns are instructed from a learner-centered perspective and are placed in a very teacher-directed classroom, they may not have the necessary skills to be flexible. University and clinical faculty must have adequate time to develop collegial relationships.

University Faculty Feedback Measures

Each week interns meet with their university faculty in *seminars*. Although the use of this seminar time varies across university faculty, common purposes of these seminars arise. Time is devoted to group reflection on individual practices, student behaviors and responses to instruction, effective teaching practices, and other issues. Interns who have taught successful lessons in school classrooms are invited to share their lessons with others in the seminars. Interns are also able to freely voice concerns about field experiences and their own doubts and fears as developing professionals. Seminars are governed by the rule, "What is said here, stays here," and communication skills such as active listening are practiced and reinforced.

Before conducting a small-group or whole class lesson, interns share their lesson plans with university faculty who *respond to those lesson plans* verbally or in writing. This feedback stimulates interns' thinking in several ways:

- strengthening parts of the lesson that may be weak

- generating alternate ways to reach the learning objectives
- anticipating parts of the lesson that may require reteaching or additional strategies
- predicting the success of the lesson

Following each observation by university faculty, *notes taken during the observation and written feedback* are shared with interns. These notes and feedback are then reviewed in *postobservation conferences.* The tone of these postobservation conferences varies according to the needs of the intern and the styles of the university faculty. *However, because the main purpose of these conferences is to promote interns' ability to reflect upon their own teaching and solve their own dilemmas of practice, it is critical to refrain from simply giving praise, criticism, or suggestions. Time must be dedicated to having interns verbally analyze their own practice and effects on students, generate alternate strategies to use, and commit to self-examination and self-improvement.* Interns and university faculty collaboratively set goals for improvement, and progress toward reaching these goals is discussed in subsequent conferences. The developmental nature of these postconferences becomes self-evident over time, as interns talk very little during the first conference but become increasingly verbal and perceptive in subsequent conferences.

Having interns *videotape* one another as they teach a lesson to a small group or whole class is a highly effective feedback procedure. The intern and university faculty then make an appointment to view the videotape as a team, stopping whenever either has a question or comment. Through watching this videotape together, the team analyzes precisely the actions and strategies of the intern, questions underlying reasons for actions, discusses student reactions, and generates alternative strategies for handling select situations. This taping affords interns a realistic and objective picture of how their behaviors and words affect their students.

Considerations for Planning Feedback

As teacher educators restructure preparation programs to include substantive early field experiences, simply increasing the time spent in the field will not necessarily improve program quality without careful attention to situational contexts in which those experiences occur. Those working in field-based settings must consider the opportunities and constraints of each site when developing activities and feedback measures. The following are important considerations:

Plan Collaboratively. The SWT-CPDT emphasizes collaborative planning at each site involving university and clinical faculty and school administrators to build a sense of shared responsibility and ownership and minimize conflicts. Team-building activities and listening to all parties' needs and concerns create an atmosphere in which all parties are considered equal and all opinions are valued and validated.

Provide Time for Planning and Dialogue Between University and Clinical Faculty. In many instances, there is an incongruency between university and clinical faculty schedules so that time for meaningful planning for feedback is limited. University and clinical faculty require time for dialogue to develop a mutual and realistic awareness of the field experience and needs of interns. At SWT-CPDT sites, interns, under the supervision of school administrators, substitute for teachers, allowing time for these discussions. Initially these weekly meetings are brief, but they lengthen as interns gain confidence and skill in handling their classes alone.

Provide Time to Meet With Interns. The reality of field-based programs is that often university faculty hurry from classroom to classroom, observing and giving feedback to many interns in a brief time frame. Such tight scheduling severely constrains the clinical supervision cycle of preobservation conferences, observation, and postobservation feedback. Field experiences must allow adequate time for this supervision cycle so that learning from experience is maximized.

Provide Meeting Space in Field Settings. Lack of space is a problem in most public schools, making it difficult for university faculty to find meeting space for debriefing interns. University

TABLE 5.1 Types of Feedback and Resource Requirements

	Degree of Resources Required		
Types of Feedback	High	Medium	Low
Daily reflection forms		X	
Intern postobservation reflections		X[a]	
Lesson repetition	X[b]		
Self-report checklist			X
Clinical faculty informal feedback		X[c]	
Lesson planning	X[d]		
Observation notes with suggestions		X[e]	
Postobservation conferences	X[f]		
Seminars	X		
Videotaping with feedback	X[g]		

a. Interns might record these reflections on audiotape rather than writing them. In situations in which high trust levels exist, interns could discuss in pairs or in small groups their reflections on the postobservation data and suggestions shared with them.

b. If time does not allow an intern to refine a lesson plan, based on experiences from teaching it a first time, and then reteach it a second time, the refined lesson plan could still be resubmitted to clinical or university faculty or to peers for feedback.

c. Rather than giving this feedback verbally or in writing, clinical faculty might find it more convenient to use electronic mail, if those capabilities are available.

d. Instead of clinical and university faculty's reviewing the lesson plans of interns, interns could serve as critical friends for one another by reviewing one another's lesson plans in pairs. Additionally, interns might individually present their lesson plans to a small group of others for suggestions for improvement.

e. Interns might be taught to observe one another, take observation notes, and use a peer coaching model to critique each other.

f. When time is limited, clinical and university faculty might give postobservation feedback in written form only. If written feedback is given, interns might reflect in a journal type of activity on the written feedback, giving clinical and university faculty an opportunity to understand the intern's perspective and respond.

g. If a high level of trust exists among interns, they might watch one another's videotapes in pairs or in small groups to give constructive criticism to each other. Individual interns could alternatively review their own videotapes alone if they were given a rubric or checklist to be used in self-assessment and reflection.

faculty must work with school administrators to find private meeting space for appropriate, productive feedback.

Consider Available Resources. The resources available at school sites exert a significant impact on the types of feedback that may be used effectively. Table 5.1 is a matrix listing SWT-CPDT feedback measures in terms of the amount of resources required for effective implementation. Those planning field experiences may avoid frustration by selecting feedback measures for which they possess adequate resources.

Conclusion

Feedback is an essential tool in helping interns develop as expert, self-reflective teachers. Careful consideration must be given to planning effective feedback that meets interns' needs. The strategies described here have been developed over time and are continually evaluated and refined. Like good teaching, an effective feedback system is flexible and enriching and, most important, helps the learner grow.

References

Berliner, D. C. (1986). In pursuit of the expert pedagogue. *Educational Researcher, 15,* 3-13.

Livingston, C., & Borko, H. (1989). Expert-novice differences in teaching: A cognitive analysis and implications for teacher education. *Journal of Teacher Education, 40,* 36-42.

Zeichner, K. M. (1980). Myths and realities: Field-based experiences in preservice teacher education. *Journal of Teacher Education, 21,* 45-55.

Evaluating Student Teachers

The Formative and Summative Process

SUSAN E. PULLMAN

Background Information

Educational reform and restructuring have caused colleges and universities to raise their admission standards for teacher education programs (Demetrulias, Chiodo, & Diekman, 1990). In a review of research on teacher selection in 1979, Schalock found the correlations between achievement measures and teaching effectiveness to be quite small; in fact, he concluded that those measures of intelligence and academic ability have not shown a consistent, strong correlation with teaching success. In a more recent study, Riggs and Riggs (1990) concluded that GPA is not a significant predictor of successful teaching performance. Along with the GPA, many institutions also use some type of standardized test score as an admission criterion. Some of the most important teaching behaviors, such as establishing and maintaining rapport with students, motivating students, and making professional decisions under complex and difficult situations, are not measured by a standardized test (Demetrulias et al., 1990).

If the GPA and standardized test are not the significant predictors of successful teaching, then what is it that is characteristic of a successful teaching program? Guidelines for assessment of teacher education programs are in a constant state of development on the university, state, and national levels. One national assessment program, the National Council for the Accreditation of Teacher Education (NCATE), requires its accrediting institutions to focus on teaching models that are grounded in research. These models provide various approaches to program assessment, one of which is to evaluate the student's performance in both clinical and field experiences. This type of program assessment is of much more concern to researchers, developers of curricula models, and groups such as NCATE; however, it is not the focus here. This chapter will focus on a more personal level of assessment, the type of assessment that will be reflective of the performance of the student teacher and indicative of his or her potential for success as a teacher.

Assessment that focuses on the student teacher's performance must give careful consideration to its supervision practices. Teacher education programs try to make every effort to assign qualified professionals to observe student teachers. Each program uses a slightly different formative assessment model. Professionals interested in gathering information on the topic of student teacher assessment can get in touch with some of the following professional organizations: Association of Teacher Educators (ATE), American Association of Colleges for Teachers Education (AACTE), Association of Supervision and Curriculum Development (ASCD), American Education Research Association (AERA), and Phi Delta Kappa (PDK). These and similar organizations, along with the learned societies, distribute publications that offer a wide range of articles, including many on student teacher assessment models. At any national, regional, or state conference a multitude of sessions are dedicated to the assessment of the students in a pre-student teaching and student teaching experience along with ongoing evaluation models of practicing teachers. Along with all of the changes in national and state standards come changes in the assessment or evaluation models used to assess performance of the student teacher or practicing teacher.

Elements of an Evaluation Model

There are three basic elements that should be taken into consideration when developing any formative evaluation instrument. First, there is the multitude of competencies or outcomes that must be considered to evaluate the various areas of teaching performance. The second is a list of descriptors to delineate the level of performance over a set period of time for each of the outcomes or competencies. It is this information that is gathered from the formative assessment instrument and is then summarized to develop a summative evaluation. Whether one is developing a formative instrument for the pre-student teacher, the student teacher, or the practicing teacher, the outcomes and level of performance will affect the tone of the instrument. The third element is a scale to define the level of performance for each of the descriptors. In the development of any assessment instrument, one must keep in perspective the purposes of the instrument, along with whom the instrument will serve. Instruments developed to evaluate the student teaching experience must not only focus on providing information on the performance level of the student teacher but also provide information on the teacher education program and provide some evidence to school administrators predicting potential teaching ability of the person evaluated by the instrument.

The Audience

A primary concern in the development of both formative and summative instruments will be to communicate to school administrators the potential performance level of the person they intend to hire. Short of nepotism, two factors have surfaced as the most important components in the recruitment and selection process. The first is the credential file, which includes evaluations from major field experiences and student teaching, and the second is the interview process (Douglas, 1983; Engle & Friedrichs, 1980; Jarchow, 1981; Natter, 1983; Yantis & Carey, 1972). As a member of a local school board for 8 years and the chief administrator of a student teaching program for 11 years, I have continually listened and responded to both board members' and administrators' concerns about the success of the candidate in the student teaching experience as a prediction of his or her teaching success in the respective school district. These exit or final evaluations should reflect in some form, regardless of whether they are open-ended or forced-choice models, performance-based criteria that include some of the most accepted indicators of a candidate's potential for being an effective teacher. Because teaching is such a complex process, there is not any "empirically verified criteria for predicting success as a teacher" (Demetrulias et al., 1990; Evertson, Hawkey, & Zlotnik, 1984). Therefore the performance-based criteria should include some of the most accepted criteria, such as love of knowledge, people, and teaching; personality characteristics that include creativity, enthusiasm, flexibility, and patience; and classroom skills that consider ability to organize and maintain a positive learning environment and use good communication skills (Evertson et al., 1984; Shanoski & Hranitz, 1989). Regardless of the instrument or form used to evaluate the student teacher, professional evaluations and recommendations are considered to be a most important element in the credential file in education (Douglas, 1983; Natter, 1983; Yantis & Carey, 1972), especially the evaluation from the cooperating teacher (Braun, Green, Willems, & Brown, 1990).

Getting Started on the
Formative Data-Gathering Instrument

Which comes first, the development of a professional education curriculum that reflects practices in "good teaching" or the research for and development of an instrument that reflects per-formance-based criteria? On one hand, if you develop an in-strument that is reflective of your program but does not reflect empirically verified criteria for predicting success as a teacher, then you run the risk of losing credibility with districts that hire your graduates, especially if the graduates are having difficulty assimilat-ing successful teaching practices into the teaching environment. However, if you develop an instrument that includes acceptable performance-based criteria of teacher effectiveness, but the instru-ment has little or no relationship to the field and course work that precede the student teaching experience, you then run the risk of setting up your students for failure. Therefore, the person devel-oping the criteria for the formative instrument should be closely involved with both the development of the curriculum in the teacher education program and the development of the instru-ment used to evaluate the program.

A review of the literature on effective teaching could consume this entire chapter. Therefore, in developing an assessment instru-ment, it is necessary to research some of the major writings on this topic. The best place to begin this research is with Dewey's con-cept of effective educational practices; then continue through the past decade of research on teaching, which has generated a knowl-edge base for effective teaching (Ayers, 1990). The need for new program models has been formulated from this knowledge base, along with the efforts of the NCATE and other professional and learned societies. This is now an ongoing process in hundreds of teacher education programs across the country. A final suggestion is to review the 19 postulates that Goodlad (1990) deemed neces-sary for an excellent teacher education program. In conclusion, the development of any instrument for evaluating the student teacher must be preceded by research on effective practices in teacher education, along with a clear understanding of and agreement with the mission statement of both the institution and teacher education program in which the instrument will be used. It is also important to mention here that the development of any instru-ment should include the collaboration of faculty, practicing teach-ers, and administrators and supervisors.

Developing the Instrument

Evaluating a student teacher's performance has two major purposes: (a) to record student progress and aid the student teacher in improving teaching skills, and (b) to provide a meaningful description of the student's teaching ability to hiring institutions. The former purpose is achieved through the use of a formative evaluation instrument to relate the student's progress during conferences held with the college supervisor(s) and cooperating teacher(s); the latter is documented at the end of the student teaching experience, using a summative evaluation form. All evaluations should lead to the most accurate answer to the question: "Does this student teacher *demonstrate* the necessary skills, attitudes, concepts, and reflective decision-making techniques required to be an effective teacher?" This is the information that concerns both school administrators who are hiring teachers and campus supervisors who are providing the gatekeeping duties of the profession. Historically, references for the student teacher have been based primarily on the student teacher's potential, with some reference to the performance level of the student teacher. Even though the student teacher may possess profound potential, evaluations during the student teaching experience must be based on actual performance to ensure credibility and accurate program assessment for the institution; therefore, it is imperative that the formative and summative report form cover several areas related to performance. A search of the literature will provide a number of character traits that most concern hiring administrators (Henjum, 1983; Murphy, 1990), along with a set of performance-based criteria that includes some of the most accepted indicators for teacher effectiveness. These indicators include (a) personality characteristics, (b) documented experience in the classroom such as planning the instruction process, (c) interest in and knowledge of teaching, (d) knowledge of subject matter and use of materials, and (e) knowledge about students and a commitment to their learning (Evertson et al., 1984). The following examples are taken from one of these most accepted indicators.

A Sample of a Formative Assessment Instrument

The first indicator will be *Personality Characteristics*. This can be expressed with a variety of headings, but all headings should make specific reference to personality characteristics. This is where your team of faculty, teachers, principals, and supervisors can play an important role. Give them the major area and then let them determine the performance criteria through a consensus-building process. The following is an example of a few items:

The Student Teacher:
- Shows fairness, tact, compassion, and good judgment in dealing with pupils.
- Reacts with sensitivity to the needs and feelings of others.
- Requests appropriate professional assistance when needed.
- Demonstrates proper listening skills.
- Follows the policies and procedures of the school district.
- Works effectively as a member of an instructional team.

Once a list of performance criteria has been established for a formative assessment instrument, a set of descriptors should be developed to designate the level of performance for each criterion. The advantage in developing these descriptors is to thoroughly understand the various levels of performance, as shown in Figure 6.1; however, the disadvantage is that the list can become very cumbersome when the teacher is trying to observe and evaluate the student teacher. In listing the descriptors it may be best to use numbers or letters that will relate to the rating scale. The following is a numerical scale with one (1) as the lowest value.

Performance criteria: Shows fairness, tact, compassion, and good judgment in dealing with pupils.

Descriptors:
1. Is unaware of needs. (level #1; poorest rating)

Directions: Select a rating number for each behavior and record it in the appropriate time period. All behaviors in a given time period should be rated

Rating Scale

NA = Not Applicable

High   Low
5   4   3   2   1

Rating Periods

Date	Optional	Midterm	Optional	Date

I. WORKING WITH PEOPLE

A. Shows fairness, tact, compassion, and good judgment in dealing with pupils.

B. Reacts with sensitivity to the needs and feelings of others.

C. Requests appropriate professional assistance when needed.

D. Demonstrates proper listening skills.

E. Follows the policies and procedures of the school district.

F. Works effectively as a member of an instructional team.

G. Other _____

Midterm Statement: Working With People

Figure 6.1. Progress Report Form With Grid

2. Is aware of the above characteristics but does not demonstrate consistency. (level #2; trying but needs constant guidance)

3. Expresses verbally the need to show fairness, tact, compassion, and good judgment in dealing with pupils. (level #3; doing okay)

4. Displays fairly consistent response patterns in dealing with pupils. (level #4; doing a fine job)

5. Displays a consistent pattern of fairness, tact, and compassion as part of the daily routine. (level #5; highest rating)

There are a variety of symbols that can be used in the development of such a scale. These symbols can include numbers such as 1, 2, 3, 4, 5; the traditional letters grades A, B, C, D, F; or a very general scale such as an "S" for satisfactory and a "U" for unsatisfactory. Another general symbol is the plus (+) , minus (–), or check (√). This last set of symbols can also be used in conjunction with the satisfactory and unsatisfactory symbols used to denote the level of performance for each descriptor.

A brief word about using letter grades as opposed to a numerical scale in the development of the formative evaluation instrument: Teachers are already influenced by the parameters of the traditional letter grades and tend to be much too generous with letter grades, giving mostly As and Bs to student teachers. Whatever type of scale is used, whether it is a set of descriptors for each performance criterion or a general scale, it must be clearly defined to all participants in the program, including the student teachers, cooperating teachers, and college supervisors. The relationship of this scale to the final grade in the student teaching course should also be well established prior to the experience and should set the tone for summative evaluation.

In developing a general scale, it is important that the levels of performance relate to each of the criteria. For the sake of setting up a sample of a general scale, we will use a numerical scale with five (5) as the highest rating and one (1) as the lowest. To assist the person who is evaluating the student teacher, it is important to develop a set of descriptors for each level related to the numerical scale. The more levels in the scale, the more difficult it becomes to define the distinction of each level. Therefore, this sample will be limited to five levels.

Starting with (5) as the highest level, the following one-word descriptors can be used to describe this level such as *Exemplary, Admirable, Outstanding, or Excellent.* What is important is to use words that clearly define the connotation of the given level. An extended definition can also be added for clarification so teachers and supervisors are consistently aware of the various levels of performance as it relates to the one-word descriptors, such as: *The student teacher who demonstrates exemplary (or whatever descriptor is used) performance for the particular criterion that is being evaluated. Performance is beyond expectation level. The student teacher is a self-starter, takes the initiative to begin work, creates own ideas, learns quickly, is well organized and resourceful, uses a variety of strategies, and shows measurable evidence of learning. The student teacher relates well with students and staff.* Because this rating is the top of the scale, the definition should outline the highest level of performance expected for that particular rating.

The next level (4) can be described as *Highly Successful.* The extended definition for this level would include: *The student teacher can function independently and is successful with classroom performance. This is evidenced by the student's performance and classroom management techniques. The student teacher is flexible and demonstrates some extra initiative most of the time.* In using the scale, cooperating teachers and campus supervisors must have confidence in the definition of each level and be able to defend their position. These descriptors are somewhat subjective; therefore the definitions need to be as tight as possible to allow the evaluator to be as objective as possible.

The scale would then proceed down to level one (1), which could be described as *Less Successful.* At this level it should be clear that: *The student teacher has little knowl-*

Working With People

A. Shows fairness, tact, compassion, and good judgment in dealing with pupils.
   1. Is unaware of needs.
   2. Is aware but does not demonstrate consistency.
   3. Expresses verbally the need to show fairness, tact, compassion, and good judgment in dealing with pupils.
   4. Displays fairly consistent response patterns.
   5. Displays a consistent pattern of fairness, tact, and compassion as part of the daily routine.
B. Reacts with sensitivity to the needs and feelings of others.
   1. Lacks show of sensitivity.
   2. Responds with sensitivity to group needs.
   3. Responds with sensitivity to group as individual ability.
   4. Responds to each individual.
   5. Responds with sensitivity to each individual needs.
C. Requests appropriate professional assistance when needed.
   1. Does not seek assistance for use of materials and equipment from colleagues when needed.
   2. Request professional assistance only after running into serious trouble in the classes.
   3. Request special assistance from immediate supervisors.
   4. Seeks professional assistance from colleagues.
   5. Seeks out appropriate professional assistance from a variety of sources.

Figure 6.2. Guidelines for a Formative Report

edge of the particular criterion being evaluated or the student teacher has performed poorly on that particular criterion.

If the general scale clearly describes the parameters of each level of performance, then it can be used efficiently, unlike the list in Figure 6.2. This extensive list of descriptors can become very cumbersome during an observation. Regardless of the format, it is important to have the cooperating teachers and college supervisors participate in the development of any formative assessment instrument, because their input can contribute to the validity of each competency as well as provide explicit guidelines for each competency.

Gathering data with an instrument so constructed is very important for the student teacher. One of the primary purposes of the data-gathering instrument is to aid the student teacher in improving his or her teaching skills. When using the formative instrument, the cooperating teacher and the college supervisor should be as open and candid as possible in their evaluation of the student teacher. The student teacher should be fully aware of the assessment model and his or her progress with reference to the evaluation instrument. Successful or outstanding performance should be both recognized and communicated, not only verbally but also formally through the formative assessment instrument. If, however, the student's performance is considered less than satisfactory, this should also be clearly communicated along with recommendations for improvement. The formative data should be used throughout the student teaching experience, with formal observations and conference sessions taking place at specific intervals. The cooperating teacher should use this formative assessment form to evaluate the student teacher approximately every 2 weeks during the entire experience so that he or she has sufficient data to write a comprehensive summative evaluation. Specific recommendations for improvement in performance should be offered by the cooperating teacher and the college supervisor. When specific recommendations are suggested, they should be dated and recorded on the assessment instrument. It is also necessary for a director of the student teaching program to provide some type of orientation for all persons involved in the student teaching experience. During this orientation student teachers must be introduced to the instrument used in the assessment process and must be apprised of the procedures for using the instrument. The orientation should also include information on the procedure and the importance of gathering data throughout the experience.

It should also be stressed that these data not only will assist both the cooperating teacher and the college supervisor in writing the final summative evaluation of the student teaching experience but will also supply important information to assist the student teacher in continual growth throughout the experience.

All of this information becomes crucial documentation. If at any time during the quarter the performance of a student teacher is determined by the cooperating teacher and/or the college supervisor to be unsatisfactory, and if the prognosis for future success is questionable, then it will be necessary to rely on the evidence previously gathered through the use of the formative instrument for diagnosing the student teacher's performance. The college supervisor can then inform the director of the student teaching program so that the necessary procedures can be initiated in the event the student teacher needs to withdraw from the student teaching experience. If for any reason an administrator from a participating school district requests that a student teacher be removed from the classroom, the necessary documentation would then be in order. This will allow the field experience director to take the necessary steps to comply with the withdrawal request and maintain a due process procedure for the student teacher. Whether the student teacher is relocated in another site or withdrawn from the student teaching program will depend on the data collected from the formative instrument by both the cooperating teacher and the campus supervisor.

It is through a written formative assessment instrument (O'Shea, 1984) that the student teachers can reflect upon their progress and learn to assess their teaching performance from constructive criticism. The use of a formative assessment instrument will not only bring greater accuracy to the summative report written by both the cooperating teacher and campus supervisor but will also allow both to use a more directive approach to supervision when necessary. There should not be any surprises for the student teacher in the final evaluation process, because all information describing the student's progress has been documented. An undocumented process of evaluation can often leave the student teacher unsure of his or her performance level because few or no diagnostic or

prescriptive techniques have been provided to improve the teaching practices until the final summative report is written or the final
grade is submitted.

Writing the Formal Summative Evaluation

Final evaluations will most likely be written by both the cooperating teacher and the college supervisor. Because the cooperating teacher will have spent an enormous amount of time working
with the student teacher, the cooperating teacher's evaluation or
recommendation can be extremely influential as part of the credential packet in delineating that fine difference between outstanding performance or highly successful performance (Braun
et al., 1990; Tracy, Sheehan, & McArdle, 1988), even more influential than a high GPA. However, that influence depends on the
quality of the final evaluation, the information contained in the
evaluation, and the tone of the evaluation. Although the cooperating teacher and college supervisor may discuss the evaluation,
each should be encouraged to write an independent report. Early
studies (Mortaloni, 1974) found that administrators responded
positively to desirable descriptors such as enthusiasm, respond-
ing to constructive criticism, cooperative attitude, and the desire
to work hard. Later studies by Evertson et al. (1984) still suggest
that potential indicators of teacher effectiveness, such as knowledge of subject, personality characteristics, interest in teaching,
and experience in the classroom, are of greater interest to administrators than test scores or the GPA.

The development of these essential performance-based criteria, along with the physical appearance of the report (e.g., typed
or handwritten), the process of saying what you mean to say, and
the tone of the summative evaluation should be reflective of the
data gathered on the formative assessment instrument during the
experience. Because the final evaluation report can affect whether
the prospective teacher will be called for an interview, it is the
responsibility of person(s) in charge of the student teaching program to inform the cooperating teachers and/or the campus supervisors of the importance of this final evaluation document as

part of the credential file. Professional development activities for cooperating teachers and campus supervisors are appropriate activities that serve this purpose.

Workshops for Cooperating
Teachers and Campus Supervisors

Because the administrators screen the credential materials of the student teachers, it has already been established that the final summative evaluation is a critical reference. Therefore *what we say, how we say it, and how the evaluation looks* are all important factors that are taken into consideration when the summative evaluation is read by administrators. Most cooperating teachers are not aware of the importance of this summative evaluation and do not realize that their own professional credibility is also on the line. It is the responsibility of the person in charge of the student teaching program to offer some type of professional development for the cooperating teachers and campus supervisors during the term they have the student teacher. This is not only an opportunity for direct contact with the cooperating teachers, to communicate the goals of the student teaching program, but also an opportunity to promote dialogue between the cooperating teacher and the campus supervisor.

In organizing any workshop for cooperating teachers and/or campus supervisors, it is important to have clear, specific objectives for the workshop that are communicated prior to the participants' attending. The workshops should be offered during the term that the teacher has the student teacher and well before the summative report is to be written. Workshop activities include such areas as a critical review of formal evaluations, an open discussion of the evaluation's strengths and weaknesses, a discussion of phrases and words that ensure that the final evaluation reflects the success (or lack of success) of the student teacher's performance, and/or the issue of performance versus the potential of the student teacher. The workshop should be organized so the participants are actively involved at all times, keeping in mind that the overall objective is to assist in the writing of the summative evaluation. The physical setup of the workshop should allow participants to be grouped around small tables (four to eight per table) to encourage conversation during the session.

As a facilitator of the workshop, it is important that you become very familiar with all the material you are using, what you will want to discuss, and how the statements in the evaluations can be made more specific to reflect what needs to be written in a final evaluation. Allow participants the opportunities to read some former evaluations and/or to write about an area regarding their own student teacher's performance. Give the participants enough time to read and discuss the sample evaluations in their small groups. During the large-group discussion, it is important to guide their comments to reflect general appearance, legibility, language structure, spelling, the style and tone of the written evaluations, and the relationship of the performance criteria in the formative assessment instrument to the written statements in the summative final evaluation. During the large-group discussion, the facilitator may wish to point out examples of how the teacher's credibility is established throughout the final evaluation. Give the group an opportunity to begin some type of writing activity, but do not be discouraged if some participants do not write. Having run these workshops for more than 10 years, I have found that by this point in the workshop, the cooperating teachers are somewhat over-whelmed by the importance of every word and phrase and are somewhat reluctant to volunteer. Keep the discussion about stu-dent performance flowing and encourage small-group participa-tion. Having trained campus supervisors attend these workshop sessions helps to ensure dialogue with and among the cooperating teachers.

A Final Word About
the Evaluation and the Recommendation

Most student teaching programs request that cooperating teachers and campus supervisors submit some type of final report summarizing the student's overall performance as part of the contractual agreement. There are some student teaching programs in which the cooperating teachers and campus supervisors must write a final evaluation, but they could also be requested by the student teacher to write an additional recommendation. The decision as to whether the evaluation and the recommendation are separate documents may be partly decided by the job planning or career service department. The cost of copying materials may limit the number of documents in a student's file. The final evaluation is the written summative report that speaks to the issue of the student's performance during the student teaching experience, based upon the formative assessment instrument. The recommendation can also be a written report that is summative of the student's performance, but the recommendation usually justifies the student teacher's potential as a successful teacher. However, both documents should be typed on a form designed for that specific purpose; the full name of the student teacher, the cooperating teacher, and the college supervisor, along with the name of the school district, building, and grade level (including the subject specialty, if necessary) are separate for the summative text. The body of the summative text should reflect some relationship to the formative assessment instrument, covering the same major areas addressed in the formative assessment instrument. If the cooperating teacher or the campus supervisor wishes to recommend the student teacher for a teaching position, that recommendation can be included in the last few lines of the summative evaluation; however, both groups should understand that the recommendation is an optional section and should not be included unless the student teacher is deserving of such a recommendation.

References

Ayers, W. (1990). Rethinking the profession of teaching: A progressive option. *The Journal of the Association of Teacher Education, 52*(1), 1-5.

Braun, J. A., Jr., Green, K., Willems, A., & Brown, M. (1990). Getting a job: Perceptions of successful applicants for teaching positions. *The Journal of the Association of Teacher Education, 52*(2), 44-54.

Demetrulias, D. M., Chiodo, J. J., & Diekman, J. E. (1990). Differential admission requirements and student achievement in teacher education. *Journal of Teacher Education, 41*(2), 66-72.

Douglas, J. B. (1983). An examination of selection procedures for professional staff in the public secondary schools of Alabama. *Dissertation Abstracts International, 43,* 3468A.

Engle, R. A., & Friedrichs, D. (1980). The emergence approach: The interview can be a reliable process. *N.A.S.S.P. Bulletin, 64*(432), 85-91.

Evertson, C., Hawkey, W., & Zlotnik, M. (1984). *The characteristics of effective teacher preparation programs: A review of research.* Washington, DC: National Commission of Excellence in Teacher Education.

Goodlad, J. (1990). *Teachers for our nation's schools.* San Francisco: Jossey-Bass.

Henjum, A. (1983). Let's select "self-actualizing" teachers. *Education, 104*(1), 51-55.

Jarchow, E. M. (1981). The hiring game. *The Clearinghouse, 54,* 366-369.

Mortaloni, R. (1974). *School administrators evaluate the letter of reference and select recruitment practices.* Madison, WI: Author. (ERIC Document Reproduction Service No. ED 099 965)

Murphy, L. (1990). Characteristics of a good teacher. *Delta Kappa Gamma Bulletin, 57*(1), 39-45.

Natter, L. F. (1983). The hiring of teachers—What principals prefer. *Small School Forum,* 12-14.

O'Shea, D. (1984). Teacher education: An empirical study of the problems and possibilities. *Journal of Education for Teaching, 10*(4), 1-23.

Riggs, I. M., & Riggs, M. L. (1990). Predictors of student success in a teacher education program: What is valid, what is not. *Action in Teacher Education, 12*(4), 41-46.

Schalock, D. E. (1979). Research on teacher selection. In D. Berliner (Ed.), *Review of research in education* (pp. 354-417). Washington, DC: American Education Research Association.

Shanoski, L. A., & Hranitz, J. R. (1989, July/August). *An analysis of characteristics of outstanding teachers and the criteria used by colleges and universities to select future teachers.* Paper presented at the Association of Teacher Education Workshop, Tacoma, WA.

Tracy, S. J., Sheehan, R., & McArdle, R. J. (1988). Teacher education reform: The implementors' reactions. *The Journal of the Association of Teacher Education, 50*(3), 14-21.

Yantis, J. I., & Carey, M. (1972). Improving teacher selection. *Journal of College Placement, 32*, 75-77.

Evaluating
Field Experience Programs

PATRICIA D. EXNER

"Student teaching was the most valuable experience I've had in my whole college career."

"I learned more from my cooperating teacher during my student teaching than I learned in all of my classes combined."

"Finally I was able to teach. And my cooperating teacher showed me how."

These comments, from student teachers' program evaluations, represent what we teacher educators often hear as our graduates exit their teacher education programs. At first glance, such statements might lead us to believe that our field experience programs

74

are providing what our students need to teach in the classrooms of the future. However, a closer look might point to a common relationship between student teacher and cooperating teacher: The cooperating teacher models and the student teacher copies, with little questioning and minimal connecting to earlier course work. Admittedly, from such a field experience there quite often emerges a beginning teacher confident in accepting the full responsibilities of teaching, having gradually assumed such responsibilities under the direct guidance of the cooperating teacher.

But do our students see connections between the theory of the campus-based classroom and the practice of the K-12 classroom as they attempt to address problems of teaching and learning? Can they apply their sense of these connections in ways that teaching and learning can occur in any classroom? Will seeing, and applying, empower them to confront the dilemmas of teaching in today's classrooms as well as those of future classrooms?

These questions address program goals. From these, we must move to a more encompassing question: To what degree do our field experiences contribute to overall program success? This should frame evaluations of field experience programs.

One University's Experience: The Traditional Program

Teacher education programs use multiple means of obtaining information regarding program quality and effectiveness. Exiting graduates frequently provide feedback on different components of their program, including field experiences. Alumni in the field respond to surveys focusing on the extent that their teacher education preparation influences their teaching practices.

These methods characterize past evaluation efforts at Louisiana State University (LSU) as faculty have attempted to assess teacher education programs. Substantive changes in program structure and focus, to be discussed later, have resulted from information obtained from these evaluations.

LSU has for several years solicited feedback through program evaluations completed by exiting traditional program graduates

TABLE 7.1 Questions Directly Related to Pre-Student Teaching and Student Teaching Field Experiences

---

Pre-Student Teaching Field Experiences

My pre-student teaching field experiences were

— sufficient in number and duration.

— helpful in preparing me for my student teaching.

— a valuable learning experience.

Opportunities to work with students from ethnic groups different from my own were adequately provided for during my pre-student teaching experiences.

---

at the end of their student teaching semester. The evaluation requests background information from each student and invites responses to questions on various components of the program: advising, specific course work, pre-student teaching field experiences, and student teaching. An open-ended narrative prompt encourages candid and specific elaborations on assessments made earlier in the evaluation and/or on any other perspectives deemed important for program improvement. Questions directly related to pre-student teaching and student teaching field experiences are presented in Table 7.1. These evaluations are kept confidential and anonymous, with composite results shared with faculty by the chair of the Department of Curriculum and Instruction.

Supplementing program evaluations are student teacher evaluations of the supervisory practices of the supervising teacher (Table 7.2) and the college coordinator (Table 7.3). The supervising teacher also evaluates the college coordinator, using a form similar to that used by the student teacher. These evaluations provide constructive feedback representing the perceptions of those with whom each worked. To ensure confidentiality, the coordinator of Teacher Education and Clinical Experiences shares, in writing, composite ratings and all comments with supervising teachers once there are four or more evaluations on file, and with individual college coordinators each semester.

The final component of the evaluation is that of the Office of Clinical Experiences, the division within the College of Education

TABLE 7.1 Continued

Student Teaching

I was

— comfortable teaching students with values different from my own.

— comfortable teaching students regardless of their previous learning experiences.

I could easily

— communicate with students regardless of their language background.

— develop the teaching strategies necessary to work with students with cultural, ethnic, and/or socioeconomic different backgrounds from my own.

— develop instructional activities to fit the reading abilities of all students.

— maintain discipline.

My student teaching experience was in a classroom that included one or more students from an ethnic group different from my own. (A) Yes (B) No

My educational program at LSU prepared me to deal with

— students of cultural backgrounds different from my own.

— classroom management.

The number of *actual teaching* hours in my student teaching was (A) sufficient (B) too many (C) too few.

The number of *observation* hours in my student teaching was (A) sufficient (B) too many (C) too few.

Student teaching was a valuable learning experience for me.

---

having responsibility for the administration and guidance of student teaching experiences. Questions in this evaluation focus on seminars offered as well as on staff efficiency and support.

Questionnaires to graduates, supplemented by dialogues in regional support sessions, provide additional feedback helpful in the assessment of the teacher education program. These focus on

TABLE 7.2 Evaluation of Supervising Teachers by Student
Teachers

Below is a list of supervisory practices. Using the following
scale, indicate the frequency of these practices evidenced by
your supervising teacher. Additionally, respond briefly in
narrative form, clarifying your rating. (Space provided for
narrative omitted here.) Mark the appropriate space with the
following:

1—Rarely // 2—Sometimes // 3—Most of the Time

My supervising teacher:

_____ I. explained reasonable expectations of student teaching
performance and provided constructive feedback
concerning my success in meeting those expectations.
Points to Consider
a. informed me specifically concerning my
responsibilities and the characteristics and
competencies by which my growth would be
evaluated.
b. offered specific, easy-to-understand suggestions
based on direct observations provided.
_____ II. provided the support necessary for the development of
effective teaching behaviors.
Points to Consider
a. created an environment that enabled me to maintain
good pupil control.
b. discussed my lesson plans with me and made
suggestions regarding methods and materials.
c. remained in the classroom enough to observe my
performance and give constructive criticism relevant
to the teaching of my lessons.

---

teaching strategies, planning and evaluation, classroom management, and availability of resources and support.

TABLE 7.2 Continued

____III. modeled effective teaching behaviors while allowing me to develop my own teaching style.
Points to Consider
   a. demonstrated characteristics of a master teacher.
   b. established a working relationship which allowed me to work with rather than *for* him or her.
   c. encouraged me to develop my own teaching style.

____IV. encouraged me to develop a sense of professionalism.
Points to Consider
   a. upheld the teaching profession as a worthy profession.
   b. held high yet reasonable standards for himself or herself and for me.
   c. encouraged me through his or her example to assume my responsibility for self-evaluation and self-improvement.

TABLE 7.3 Effectiveness of the College Coordinator by the Student Teacher

---

Please indicate for categories I and II whether the behavior was demonstrated. Make additional comments as appropriate. (Space provided for narrative omitted here.)

	Performance of Coordinator	
I. **Teaching Experience:** Based on the performance of the college coordinator, do you feel that he or she		
A. has had successful teaching experience?	Yes	No
B. is well prepared in content and teaching methods for coordinating in *this* teaching area and level?	Yes	No

(Continued)

TABLE 7.3 Continued

II. **Availability:** The college coordinator
    A.   made regular visits to the classroom (a   Yes   No
         minimum of five visits should be made).
    B.   made additional visits when needed or   Yes   No
         requested.
    C.   gave advance notice of most visits.   Yes   No
    D.   provided means for communicating   Yes   No
         between visits (office hours, phone
         numbers).

Listed below are criteria for judging the effectiveness of your
college coordinator. Please respond to each item. The scale at
the right is for you to indicate to what extent the behavior was
performed. Please feel free to make additional comments as
appropriate in the blanks provided.

Rate the coordinator as Very Weak   1   2   3   4   5   Very Strong

                                              Performance of
                                                Coordinator

III. **Conferencing:** The college coordinator
    A.   conducted a conference with the student   1 2 3 4 5
         teacher during each visit
    B.   scheduled sufficient time for the   1 2 3 4 5
         conference
    C.   based the conference primarily on
         1. observation of teaching performance   1 2 3 4 5
         2. constructive feedback of the student   1 2 3 4 5
             teacher's performance
    D.   conducted sufficient conferences with   1 2 3 4 5
         the supervising teacher

IV. **Human Relations/Communication:**
    The college coordinator
    A.   established and maintained good   1 2 3 4 5
         rapport with the supervising teacher,
         the student teacher, and the principal

TABLE 7.3 Continued

			Performance of Coordinator
	B.	indicated genuine interest in the student teacher	1 2 3 4 5
	C.	was tactful in speech and action	1 2 3 4 5
	D.	demonstrated leadership	1 2 3 4 5
	E.	was consistent in his or her requirements	1 2 3 4 5
V.	**Evaluation:**		
	A.	Observation of Classroom Teaching: The college coordinator	
		1. observed at regular intervals	1 2 3 4 5
		2. observed for a sustained period—at least a full period in the secondary classroom and a teaching episode or activity in the elementary classroom	1 2 3 4 5
		3. observed in different classes and/or teaching situations	1 2 3 4 5
	B.	Constructive Criticism: The college coordinator	
		1. provided *specific* oral and/or written feedback about the student teacher's performance	1 2 3 4 5
		2. used a positive approach	1 2 3 4 5
		3. suggested appropriate recommendations of teaching and classroom management techniques	1 2 3 4 5
	C.	Objectivity: The college coordinator	
		1. used performance as the primary basis for evaluation	1 2 3 4 5
		2. used observation in varied teaching situations as the primary indicator of performance	1 2 3 4 5

(Continued)

TABLE 7.3 Continued

	Performance of Coordinator
3. used recorded data (checklists, observation notes, notes from conferences with the supervising teacher, written lesson plans, written unit plans) as a basis for recommendations	1 2 3 4 5
4. identified specific weaknesses	1 2 3 4 5
VI. **Expectations:** The college coordinator	
A. clearly communicated his or her requirements and performance expectations to the student teacher and the supervising teacher	1 2 3 4 5
B. made appropriate adjustments in expectations and requirements to accommodate the needs of the student teacher and teaching situation	1 2 3 4 5
C. set high standards for the student teacher	1 2 3 4 5

Transition From Traditional Programs to Holmes Programs

Combined, these evaluations have allowed LSU faculty to assess overall program effectiveness. Student and alumni comments have pointed to a need for increased depth and breadth of course work, more extensive and diverse field experiences, and stronger connections between the two. In response, the college has begun a phaseout of traditional 4-year programs, with a phasing in of Holmes graduate programs.

Now all elementary education students enroll as juniors in a 5-year integrated program, culminating in a Master's in Education degree and teacher certification. They take additional course work in each academic area, plus they obtain the equivalent of an academic concentrate. Secondary/K-12 students enter the program with baccalaureate degrees and must complete a 15-month graduate-level program to receive a Master's in Education degree and teacher certification. The rigorous graduate year for both groups consists of course work interrelated with fall and spring practica experiences.

Within a cohort frame, students work in pairs in field experiences focusing on reflective teaching and teacher research. University and public school faculties collaborate as cohort faculty teams in integrating these field experiences with course work. The cohort team structure—based on content area certification, academic concentrate or grade level focus, research interest—allows for frequent and open dialogue resulting in immediate modification as needed.

A key player on the cohort faculty team is the clinical faculty member, a new position in the college. Clinical faculty have primary responsibility for guiding students in building connections between field experiences and course work, practice, and theory.

These changes in program structure and goals are reflected in evaluation efforts. Both formal and informal evaluation of the effectiveness of cohort team members and of the integrated program are ongoing and continuous. Formative and summative evaluations of students, some of which stem from reflective self-evaluations, allow each faculty team to assess and modify regularly on both a cohort and an individual basis.

Student evaluations of the effectiveness of clinical faculty practices, using a form created collaboratively by clinical faculty, have also resulted in modifications within individual cohorts (Table 7.4). These evaluations are kept confidential: the Coordinator of Teacher Education and Clinical Experiences shares composite results with each clinical faculty and with the department chair.

The field experiences component is evaluated at the end of the program as an integral part of the teacher education program, rather than as separate and distinct from other components (Table 7.5).

Additional feedback is solicited directly from recent Holmes graduates now teaching in the field and from their administrators. Responses to questions related to teaching success in relation to program goals have provided further information helpful in judging program effectiveness.

TABLE 7.4 Assessment of Clinical Faculty

This form is designed to provide you with an opportunity to assess the effectiveness of clinical faculty. The information you provide, particularly in narrative comments, will allow your clinical faculty to refine efforts to make the Holmes experience meaningful. Respond to each item using the scale below.

SA Strongly Agree/**A** Agree/**D** Disagree/**SD** Strongly Disagree

My Clinical Faculty

_____ 1. communicated clearly goals, expectations, and requirements for my successful completion of the clinical experience.

_____ 2. provided helpful and effective feedback after observing my teaching.

_____ 3. helped me draw upon course work in preparing for and teaching during the field experience.

_____ 4. engaged in useful and meaningful discussions with me and the public school teacher(s) with whom I worked.

_____ 5. was available to assist me in planning and preparing lessons when I requested help.

_____ 6. aided me when I requested assistance in locating resources for my teaching and research.

_____ 7. consistently encouraged me to reflect upon my own teaching practices.

_____ 8. helped me, through feedback and questioning, broaden and deepen my understanding of teaching and learning.

_____ 9. helped me to understand better classroom problems or situations through suggestions, questions, strategies, and observations.

_____ 10. understands teaching and learning, and the particular and general nature of the constraints and conditions under which teachers teach.

_____ 11. guided me in the development and pursuit of my research questions when appropriate.

_____ 12. provided feedback throughout my research when appropriate.

TABLE 7.4 Continued

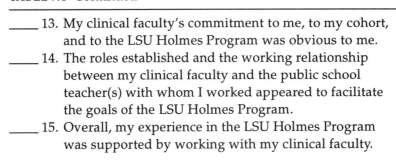

_____ 13. My clinical faculty's commitment to me, to my cohort, and to the LSU Holmes Program was obvious to me.

_____ 14. The roles established and the working relationship between my clinical faculty and the public school teacher(s) with whom I worked appeared to facilitate the goals of the LSU Holmes Program.

_____ 15. Overall, my experience in the LSU Holmes Program was supported by working with my clinical faculty.

Provide additional comments you feel may be useful in assessing the work performance of your clinical faculty. Include any suggestions regarding ways your clinical faculty might have been of greater benefit to you, to your cohort, or to your public school teacher. Also include any special strengths you feel your clinical faculty has brought to the LSU Holmes Program.

Summary

These evaluation procedures and tools represent the attempts of one teacher education institution to help its students become teacher leaders in tomorrow's classrooms. Substantive changes in program goals and structure have resulted in the integration of field experience programs with other teacher education components. Regular and systematic evaluations by students currently enrolled, by university and K-12 faculty team members, and by graduates and their employers continue to produce program change.

Change is healthy. A cliché? Perhaps. But if we want to pay more than lip service to the goal of enabling beginning teachers to apply what they know about teaching and learning to the problems encountered in the classroom, we must provide field experiences that offer multiple opportunities to do so. To do this, we must guide our students in connecting their course work and their field experiences. We cannot assume that they will make these

TABLE 7.5 LSU Holmes Program Evaluation

This instrument is divided into four sections. Section One deals with various components and features of the program. Section Two deals with program goals and objectives. Section Three deals with reflective practice. Section Four is completely open-ended.

SECTION ONE: For each of the following program components and features, tell us what we need to know based on your personal experience. Include also your assessment of this component or feature for others in your cohort and for others in the program overall. (Space provided for narrative omitted here.)

Curriculum and Course Organization
>   (the way courses—including field experiences—were scheduled, sequenced, integrated, etc.)

Relevance and Utility of Specific Courses
>   (Which courses were most valuable to you? Why? Least valuable? Why?)

The Research Project Procedures
>   (including preparation, contribution of project to your learning, oral examination, etc.)

Support Services
>   (advising, information, services, and assistance to you while in the program)

Work in Professional Development Schools
>   (administrative support, the August experience, overall preparation, the idea of working with a peer partner, working in multiple schools/with more than one teacher, expectations, support for research project, etc.)

Methods of Assessment
>   (fall midsemester self-evaluation shared with peer and faculty team, faculty team evaluation at end of first semester and at spring midsemester, self-evaluation at end of spring semester)

TABLE 7.5 Continued

Faculty Roles

(assessments of how your clinical faculty, graduate faculty mentors, and public school teachers worked together and independently to help you succeed in the program)

**Clinical faculty

**Graduate faculty mentor

**Public school teachers

**Teamwork, coordination, joint planning between/among the above

SECTION TWO: Your program has been designed to center your reflection and learning on the following six areas. Before offering elaborated comments about the program's *overall* success in regard to each, use the following scale to help us see our relative success in each area:

Place a "4" in the blank if the program was especially successful for you in this area;

"3" if the program was generally successful;

"2" if the program was only somewhat successful;

"1" if the program was rarely if at all successful.

___ Epistemology (understanding of knowledge and its broad implications for teaching and learning, multiple ways of knowing). Comments:

___ Schooling and Education (historical and philosophical traditions, social/political/economic context). Comments:

___ Content (specific discipline/subject, curriculum decision making, intervention strategies). Comments:

___ Learning and Learners (mainstreamed and not mainstreamed; development, needs of culturally diverse learners). Comments:

___ Research (assumptions about knowledge, modes of inquiry, research/practice relationships, etc.). Comments:

___ Profession (ethics, policy issues, professional renewal, etc.). Comments:

TABLE 7.5 Continued

SECTION THREE: Throughout the program, we have tried to assist you in your development toward reflective practice—a process of critical inquiry, analysis, decision making, and evaluation. We have tried to make reflection integral to all program components. Use the space below to assess how successful the program has been in helping you become reflective in your practice.

SECTION FOUR: What else would you like to tell us about the program so that we can continue to make it better?

---

connections on their own; if they do, it will probably be accidental and later on.

If we equate success in the classroom with the ability to assess and modify instruction on an ongoing basis, why then should we not use the same standard for teacher education programs? As we evaluate our field experiences programs, we should ensure that these evaluations remain within the context of the whole teacher education program. Before determining the effectiveness of field experiences in providing what our students need to teach in tomorrow's classrooms, we must determine what our teacher education program defines as those needs. Once we have determined these program goals, we can begin our evaluation.

Assessment of field experiences as one of the interrelated components of a teacher education program should focus on the degree that the experiences contribute to overall program success. Only then can we look with optimism toward the prospects for the classrooms of tomorrow.

❖ 8 ❖

Operating a Small Field
Experience Program for Teacher
and Administrator Preparation
in a Private School of Education

BARBARA ANN COULIBALY
RITA M. KING

The University of the Pacific (UOP) has its main campus in Stockton, California, in a county of more than one-half million persons. It is one of the richest agricultural counties in the United States and a major port facility that is becoming one of California's primary links to the Pacific Rim trade and world market.

Founded in 1851, UOP is the oldest charter institution of higher learning in California. It accommodates approximately 4,000 students annually from more than 40 states and more than 60 foreign countries. The Gladys L. Benerd School of Education, home to approximately 457 students in the 1992-1993 school year, enjoys a reputation in California as being approved by the National Council for the Accreditation of Teacher Education (NCATE) from its bachelor's through doctoral programs.

Small field experience programs are complex to handle, and this chapter will explore two emphases. The first part deals with students in the teacher education program. It examines the field experience component as it relates to student development, while describing how the field experience component functions with the issues it encounters to support its operation.

The second part reflects upon the model of having a two-tiered field experience program for persons earning an administrative credential in California. Currently, this model, in effect since 1985, is changing. The section will describe problems faced in being a small field experience program; inspect the thinking that has identified the need for changes, new directions that will be in place by 1997; and explore how a school of education will seek to best accommodate those new field experience directions.

Operating a Teacher Education
Field Experience Program Solo

The underlying assumption of the basic teacher education program at UOP is that teaching is a complex activity. The students must not only be competent in the subject matter and pedagogical knowledge and skills but also be able to respond to new situations as the need arises. Therefore, our task in the teacher preparation program is to prepare students who are able to meet the needs of their students and the school community.

The initial course work in the teacher preparation program is taught by faculty who are at the forefront of their respective fields within the liberal arts curriculum and are skillful master teachers. Most classes are relatively small, and many of the courses use activities and hands-on materials that enhance the understanding of the theoretical constructs being studied. Additionally, most of the courses include field activities that allow the student to practice in incremental steps. "Early field experiences seem to be associated with cognitive gains in professional coursework and better pre-student teaching" (Cruickshank, 1990). Students also demonstrate competency through the use of portfolios, interactive journals, and on-line interactions with faculty and with other student teachers, as well as through the use of traditional research papers, tests, and presentations.

At UOP, one of our primary goals for student teachers is for students to become reflective practitioners. They learn more about their craft and improve their instruction and their interactions with students as they engage in the field experience and reflection process. According to Tom Russell, "reflection-in-action consists of two crucial elements: *reframing*, seeing a situation in a new way as a result of unexpected messages from practice; and *new action*, a new approach to practice suggested by the reframing." One might say the reflection comes as a result of the action (Munby & Russell, 1989).

The professional education sequence at UOP provides a thorough knowledge base for students. The primary goal is to produce reflective, caring, and capable teachers who possess the knowledge and skills to meet the needs of students in our society. Courses included in this sequence include:

Foundations for teaching*

Learning and the learner*

Social studies curriculum (multiple subject)*

Math/science curriculum (multiple subject)*

Reading/language curriculum (multiple and single subject)*

Planning, organizing, and evaluating (single subject)

Instructional strategies (single subject)

* *courses that include a fieldwork component*

The final courses in the basic teacher preparation program are Directed Teaching and the Directed Teaching Seminar. The director of student teachers and interns is responsible for the placement of student teachers and interns, for both multiple subject and single subject preparation; the weekly seminar; and the assignment and supervision of university supervisors. Between 8 and 10 university supervisors are selected from school of education faculty and graduate assistants from the school of education. The supervisors visit assigned students approximately 8 to 10 times per semester.

The number of student teachers ranges from around 45 to 65. Student teachers complete the assigned experience during a 16-week semester. Single subject students are assigned at least two master teachers and two grade levels in one school. Multiple subject students are assigned to two schools and two grade levels, primary (K-3) and intermediate (4-6). Interns complete the internship during a period of one school year.

There are three school districts close to UOP: The Stockton Unified School District, serving approximately 34,000 students; Lodi Unified School District, serving more than 25,000 students; and Lincoln Unified School District, serving more than 8,000 students. Most of the student teachers and many of the interns are placed in these districts, because the schools are within a 25-mile radius of the university.

Presently, the Stockton environs is an area rich in cultural and ethnic diversity. The ethnic makeup comprises Southeast Asians and other Asian groups including Filipino, Japanese, and Chinese Americans; Mexican Americans; African Americans; and Americans of European ancestry. During the current school year, the Stockton Unified School District documented at least 28 languages within the city schools. With this diverse backdrop, UOP students have an excellent, albeit challenging, opportunity to practice in a microcosm that is said to be the prototype for the rest of the nation by the 21st century (National Public Radio, 1990). One of the challenges for the director of student teachers is to develop a close working relationship with the school districts, the school site administrators, and the teachers who are the most appropriate models for the student teachers.

In addition to selecting the most appropriate master teachers, it is also necessary to ascertain the finest match between student teachers and master teachers based on other factors. For instance, age, gender, prior experiences of student teachers, personality, and temperament are all factors that need to be considered when placing student teachers. Currently, many adults are returning to the university as a result of shifts in the job market or because of midlife career changes. Even though the student teacher is a novice in the field of education, the person may be a mature individual, with well-developed skills and knowledge in other fields. Therefore, it is essential to place those older students with an outstanding teacher who will be respectful of the student teacher's maturity and past accomplishments. The most appropriate match usually occurs when students have an opportunity to engage in field experiences, or to work with specific teachers with whom they have had contact in the past.

When the relationship between student teacher and master teacher works well, it sets a positive tone for the beginning career of the new teacher. Often the master teacher is a source of support and encouragement for years to come, and lasting friendships and relationships develop. The master teacher may become a mentor for the new teacher, and the model set by the master teacher often is of more consequence than the theoretical constructs learned in formal course work.

After each placement, students are polled for their impressions and feedback about their master teachers, the school site administrator, and the culture of the school. This data is compiled, analyzed, and used for subsequent placements. Additionally, master teachers and school site administrators are also polled for information.

In spite of the enormity of the task of director of student teachers and interns, most often it is a very rewarding and rich experience. The benefits far outweigh the problems. It is a very personalized process, and we have the opportunity to know the master teachers and site administrators well. The associations that develop between university faculty and master teachers are also often long lasting, and the relationships that grow out of our interactions with students are equally rewarding and lasting. The conflicts or challenges that occasionally arise do so because we are a small program and the amount of time involved for the director of student teachers and interns is demanding.

It is possible to meet frequently with each student teacher in the program. When students are successful, one feels very much a part of their success. Even if a student discovers that teaching is not the career for him or her, the relationship is strong enough to assist the student in finding a new direction and a more appropriate vocation.

Operating a Small
Administrative Field Experience Program

Clinical or field based experiences are prominent in the recommendations of all groups searching for improved preparation of school administrators (National Association of Elementary School Principals, 1990; National Commission on Excellence in Educational Administration, 1988; National Policy Board for Educational Administration, 1989). However, simply mandating fieldwork, practicum, internship, clinical experience, or field experience without also describing the nature of that experience does not ensure quality for the student involved.

In California, licensure of school administrators, just as with teachers, rests with the California Commission on Teacher Credentialing (CTC). As the policy-making body that establishes and maintains standards for the education profession in California, the CTC is legally responsible for all aspects of preparation, assessment, and certification of school administrators (Bartell & Birch, 1993).

In 1985 a two-level administrative credential structure was fully implemented in California, which is 1 of 27 states that have two or more levels of certification (Silhanek, 1991). A Preliminary Services Credential provides special focus in both the course work and planned field experiences to students considering going into educational administration, and the professional credential requires continued professional growth through advanced credential requirements.

Field experience for the Preliminary Services Credential necessitates performance of most major duties and responsibilities authorized by the credential in at least two school levels (elementary, junior high/middle school, or high school) along with a substantial part of fieldwork at sites where at least 20% of the students are of an ethnic/racial group different from the candidate.

The UOP educational administration program has two full-time faculty members available to assist students. Students receive individual ongoing assistance in setting up their fieldwork assignments along with visitations from the full-time faculty at the school. The full-time faculty members meet with the student and with the district supervisor who is assisting them on-site.

The Preliminary Level Field Experience currently involves an integrated program model in which the student spends time working in two experiences, doing activities that relate to the competency domains. Students organize experiences of educational leadership in two school levels and state specific tasks or projects in which they were involved. Currently, an individualized preparation program, including the field experience component, is collaboratively developed for all candidates by their adviser, in consultation with the candidates and designees of the employing school district of the candidate.

The Professional Level Credential is undergoing major revision. Presently, there are four courses, along with four field experiences, that represent eight competency areas forming the core of the Professional Tier program (Bartell & Birch, 1993) and they are required for completion of the credential. Each field experience matches the course being taken.

There are several ongoing problems that arise because of having a small Educational Administration Field Experience Program. These include the following:

- There are a multitude of districts, and frequently the field experience will be on a one-time basis with a district. Setting up a working relationship becomes new for every one of those districts.
- Students doing their field experience work with UOP often cover a wide geographical area; their school may be 100 miles or more from the university.
- The norm is having only one person from a district doing field experience work at any time.

- Because of the small numbers of field experience students in any given semester, it is difficult to host ongoing seminars for students.
- There is no cohort of students who go through the fieldwork.

Beginning in 1996, the fieldwork component will be configured differently. Because UOP has a small educational administrator preparation program, meetings with former and current students, school district personnel, district personnel directors, and our advisory committee were conducted to discuss how best to reorganize our program. One aspect of the fieldwork will be known as an "induction" program for new administrators. Prior to taking course work, newly hired administrators will meet with a university and district adviser to organize a plan for their Professional Tier Program, including a mentoring component for the candidate.

In May 1994 our department conducted an anonymous sample survey and also interviewed several students who are either currently involved in or have recently completed the Preliminary Tier Fieldwork Program. Respondents thought the field experience program allowed for flexibility and that it had a "significant impact" on them. All but two felt that it stretched them to learn new information "beyond [their] comfort zone."

Important insights occurred in the open-ended responses to two questions that specifically dealt with factors relating to the small size of the administrative fieldwork program. The first question asked about factors in the field experience program that are supportive to the candidate. Responses included the following:

- Competency guidelines
- Two-level requirement (elementary, middle, high school)
- Adviser's advice, counsel, and regular contact
- Knowledge gained from UOP administration courses
- Hands-on experience with different facets

- Flexibility to design program
- Supportive district contact

The second question invited students to discuss factors in their field experience program that they did not perceive as supporting them. Only two responses were made:

- Time. Trying to complete all requirements in one semester and teach. Fieldwork should start at the same time as the program with tie-in or emphasis with class work.
- Need for some seminars dedicated to the field experience.

In redesigning the field experience program for the Preliminary Services Credential, our department is exploring the idea of incorporating the field experience over a 12-month period, during which students also would take the majority of their course work. Several persons encouraged expanding the length of time for fieldwork in the Preliminary Tier program.

Conclusion

A small school of education has to organize its resources carefully to perform well the many details and facets related to its field experience efforts. There needs to be a positive creative tension in the field experience preparation of teachers and administrators so that they have the opportunity to learn both what is and what can be. Unless the university prepares its students by helping them develop strong connections with districts during their field experience activities, and stretches them to examine their mental models of reality so that they become reflective practitioners, university field experiences are not being comprehensive enough for the candidate, for the district, for the future of these upcoming teachers and administrators, and for the students they will serve.

References

Bartell, C. A., & Birch, L. W. (1993). *An examination of the preparation, induction, and professional growth of school administrators.*
Sacramento, CA: Commission on Teacher Credentialing.

Cruickshank, D. R. (1990). *Research that informs teachers and teacher
educators.* Bloomington, IN: Phi Delta Kappa Educational Foundation.

Munby, H., & Russell, T. (1989). Educating the reflective teacher:
An essay review of two books by Donald Schön. *Journal of
Curriculum Studies, 21*(1), 71-80.

National Association of Elementary School Principals. (1990). *Principals for 21st century schools.* Alexandria, VA: Author.

National Commission on Excellence in Educational Administration. (1988). *Leaders for America's schools.* Tempe, AZ: The University Council for Educational Administration.

National Policy Board for Educational Administration. (1989).
*Improving the preparation of school administrators: An agenda for
reform.* Charlottesville: University of Virginia.

National Public Radio. (1990, July). "America in the future." *All
Things Considered.*

Silhanek, B. (1991). *An examination of certification and professional
development of superintendents and principals across the fifty·states.*
Tama, IA: Wise Enterprises.

Coordinating Theory With Practice

The Department Chair's Perspective

MILDRED E. KERSH

Faculty in education strive to develop teacher preparation programs that integrate program goals, course activities, and the expectations of all participants into a cohesive whole. Goodlad, Soder, and Sirotnik (1990) identify five characteristics of those teacher preparation programs that achieve significant integration of program elements:

1. Preservice teacher education is the major focus of the educational unit.
2. Every faculty member is involved in the program.
3. Faculty remain in proximity to one another.
4. Faculty communicate daily and conduct serious discussions of current educational issues.

    5. The number of teachers produced annually is small.

Goodlad et al. found such programs rare, but in their study, as in most other studies on teacher preparation, the one element identified by student teachers and, on reflection, by all teachers as the most salient program feature was the student teaching experience. Academic teaching fields, education courses, and early field experiences all dim in the imperative of student teaching. As the chair of a department responsible for the total education program of teacher preparation, the impact of student teaching has been a puzzlement for me. Its importance to student teachers raises questions concerning the role student teaching could or should have in the overall program of teacher education. Should student teaching remain a driving force in teacher preparation to the extent that it becomes the entire program? That is, should teacher preparation return to an apprentice program conducted in schools, where teachers in training learn while they teach? Do preservice teachers learn best by doing? Or can we harness some of the dynamics of student teaching to invigorate university courses, thus employing student teaching as the continuing cohesion of all that teacher preparation undertakes?

    It is this latter role that can best serve teacher education as a profession. For student teaching to assume such a role, its procedures and perspectives must relate to the overall perspective of the program. Student teaching would then focus on the interconnectedness of all segments of teacher education.

    There is no one set of goals for teacher education. Programs must vary from institution to institution to accommodate university students, school conditions, and learners. There are, however, three major perspectives on the goals for teacher education. First is what may be called the "education in a box" perspective. In this view, the function of programs of teacher education is to supply preservice teachers with kits of games, activities, and materials needed for survival in student teaching and for the first years of initial certification. Supposedly, preservice teachers also learn how to create "boxes" or lessons, which they will continue to develop in the future. In this perspective, the role of student teaching is a pilot use of "the box."

The "set of skills" approach to teacher preparation assumes that the teaching act consists of a known and finite repertoire of strategies and skills that can be taught by professors, learned by students, and applied to various content. These skills are generalizable across all content. The role of student teaching is to apply learned skills to a specific classroom setting.

Yet a third, though doubtlessly there are more, perspective on the goal for teacher education is to establish a dialogue on the teaching/learning symbiosis. The dialogue initially exists between student and professor in the form of interaction through courses, mentorships, independent study, and field supervision. In large, systematized programs this dialogue is rarely developed and exists for only a few persistent students.

Dialogue is more likely nurtured in small teacher education programs and may be the reason Goodlad et al. (1990) reported small programs as achieving significantly more integration of program elements.

During student teaching the dialogue is mainly between student and supervising teacher. In most programs this is the first one-on-one dialogue the student has experienced. Personal mentorship and resulting dialogue, together with the field setting, may combine to contribute to the salience of the student teaching experience.

When reflection is practiced, there also exists a self-dialogue that should continue throughout the teacher's professional life. As the student teacher moves into the education profession, the dialogue expands to include colleagues discussing current educational issues, problem cases, successes, and innovations.

In a qualitative evaluation of one preservice program, intimations of the first two perspectives on goals for teacher preparation programs were found. Those just entering teacher education said that the goal of the program was to provide them with the materials to be good teachers. Those in student teaching stated that the goal of the program was to teach them a set of skills and how to apply those skills to be successful with learners (Scheffler, Richmond, Kersh, & Dana, 1991).

Often the procedures of student teaching are dictated by the assessment procedures mandated by agents outside the university/

college domain. In the past decade state education agencies have developed or identified specific assessment instruments for evaluating teachers. The assessment mandates have been extended to teachers in training during their full-time teaching experience. Generally encompassing such features as planning, implementing, and evaluating the effects of a series of lessons, these assessments often assume such a significance to the student that the assessment procedures dictate program elements for teacher education. For example, special courses are offered on the assessment instrument itself. Components of the instrument, judging criteria, protocol lessons, and even videotapes are taught as courses, or within courses, to ensure passing performance on the teacher assessment instrument while student teaching. In Mississippi, public university teacher education programs are accountable for the performance of program graduates during their first year evaluations on the state's mandated teacher assessment instrument. Under Standard 9 of the Standards for Performance Review of the State of Mississippi, 90% of the graduates of an institution's teacher education program who receive provisional certification must receive standard certification status after the first provisional review in order for the institution to remain on approved status (Mississippi Teacher and Administrator Education, Certification, and Development, 1990).

States persist in regulating teacher assessment in spite of increasing evidence that mandated observation instruments impose a predetermined set of values on what is acceptable practice. Those values are too often minimal in nature. Moreover, the weakest education programs are the ones most likely to be shaped by such mandated assessments (Goodlad et al., 1990).

Closely aligned to student teaching, but less often regulated, are other field experiences and clinical teaching. These often help to integrate education course content with practice. As a side effect, they occasionally serve as a filter for students who early on find that teaching is not their chosen profession. Early field experience should not supplant student teaching in which preservice teachers assume major responsibility for a group of learners for an extended, full-time experience. Field-based experiences for teachers are likely to be beneficial only under conditions of close supervision, critical inquiry into current practices, and, ultimately, residence in exemplary, renewing schools (Goodlad et al., 1990).

Even when programs include early experiences, the student teaching experience remains of greatest importance and concern to the preservice teachers. Why does student teaching assume such importance in the perceptions of preservice teachers? Are university courses so theoretical as to be bereft of practice? It is more likely that student teaching is a taste of the preservice teacher's future life. Even when a program is field-based, the most interesting part is with learners in classes.

In one field-based program with which I was associated, preservice teachers were so field-oriented that even university course assignments, designed to allow students to practice in a field setting those skills being learned in their university courses, were neglected to allow interns more time to assist teachers in "real work." The university faculty resorted to changing course grading from Pass/Fail to A-F grades to divert some of the interns' attention back to course demands.

The situation of university courses vying with field reality is the same in both education and medicine. Neither premed nor medical classes are as exciting or real as actual clinic experiences. Yet, in any profession, the most useful knowledge is theoretical.

The teacher who successfully teaches "Plan A" to a class or a student must know why it was successful to determine whether to modify, or what to modify, for future use. Knowing why a plan, an activity, or a total curriculum is a success (or a failure) is as important as knowing it was successful.

Knowing the rationale, the context, and the theory of successful learning experiences requires reflection on that experience. Student teachers should understand they will learn not from experience but from reflection on that experience. Teacher preparation programs must demand reflection on practice so frequently that it becomes a habit of teaching.

The habit of reflection is not, however, a preeminent concern expressed by student teachers. Preservice teachers are very much concerned about pupil control and classroom discipline (Coates & Thorenson, 1976; Evans & Tribble, 1986; Kazelskis, Reeves-Kazelskis, & Kersh, 1993; Veenman, 1984). They are also concerned about dimensions of self (e.g., personal efficacy, interpersonal relationships), tasks (e.g., lesson planning, assessing students' work), and impact (e.g., motivating students, teaching efficacy) (Kazelskis, Reeves-Kazelskis, & Kersh, 1991).

Elementary and secondary teachers differ in their concerns about teaching. Elementary preservice teachers express greater concern about the impact of their teaching, such as sustaining positive school climate, being accepted by students, and maintaining high classroom performance (Kazelskis et al., 1991), than did secondary preservice teachers. It is paradoxical that although they're more concerned about these impacts, elementary teachers also rated their preparation to teach higher than did secondary students, who express less concern about the impacts of their teaching. One may conclude that, regardless of the amount of preparation in some areas, preservice teachers will always express great concern over these areas; in other words, they will never feel that they have received *enough* preparation in some areas.

What is the impact of the student teaching experience on the student teachers? Hoy and Woolfolk (1990) found that student teachers became more controlling in their perspectives as they completed their practice teaching, more custodial in pupil-control orientation as well as more controlling in their orientation toward social problem solving, and less confident that they could overcome the limitations of home environment and family background.

The cooperating teachers induct the student teachers into their ways of teaching and dealing with students (Goodlad et al., 1990). Bolin (1990), using a case study approach over two semesters of student teaching, reports that the student studied became less reflective about his teaching experience as he progressed through student teaching. Katz and Raths (1982) suggest that a need to know develops during student teaching. Student teachers are frustrated by the realization that they do not have immediate solutions for real problems of real learners. Student teachers may fail to recognize university course theory as applying to a specific learner's problem. University course knowledge is retained as "inert" information by students who fail to see its relevance for classroom practice (Bransford, Vye, Adams, & Perfetta, 1989). During the student teaching experience, their need to know surges, but they are often unable to connect inert information to the immediate situation.

In summary, student teachers, as a result of the student teaching experience, become more positive about their own personal teaching efficacy but less positive about general teaching efficacy. One way the department chair can ease the trauma of beginning student teaching is to be aware of the expressed concerns of students entering student teaching and attempt to alleviate those concerns. This must be tempered with the realization that student teaching is a stressful time of trial, of constant supervision, and of evaluation, which no amount of university preparation will completely eliminate.

Despite this inevitable tension, the department chair must put in place ways to monitor the student teaching experience to ensure that the program can be modified to accommodate weaknesses. The department chair must retain a way to evaluate this crucial program phase.

Another persistent question of the department chair is who the university agent should be during the student teaching interval. Should university professors who offer courses in the program also be responsible for student teaching supervision? Or should there be a professional cadre of supervisors focused on this one phase of the program?

Historically, teacher education faculty were the original field supervisors. As teacher education evolved into the mainstream of a university, the teacher education faculty were swept into the ethos of merit and reward for teaching, service, and scholarly productivity. Student teaching is time-consuming and largely unrewarding for university faculty. A new cadre of student teaching supervisors, usually adjunct to the program, emerged to serve as university representatives to the schools where student teachers were assigned. Seldom are these student teaching staff members tenure-track professors holding faculty positions within the teacher preparation department. Often they are former teachers, usually cited for outstanding abilities in teaching. One benefit to having a professional student teaching staff is that they, as immediate-past teachers, are more readily accepted by cooperating teachers in the schools where student teachers are placed. The cooperating teachers are initially less threatened by adjunct staff and may, therefore, be more willing to accept a student teacher and the ensuing details and extra work that accompany a student teacher.

Although many teachers will confess an initial reluctance to having a university professor observing in their classroom, some have reported overcoming this reluctance and developing a collegial relationship with university professors. Mutual benefit in terms of participating in research, coauthoring papers and professional conference sessions, and being encouraged to continue graduate study are only a few of the benefits they name. Teachers also view having a student teacher, and the opportunity to interact with university professors, as a relief to the loneliness of the act of teaching.

A professional cadre is more likely to accept conditions as they are presented, rather than objecting on philosophical or professional beliefs. For example, mandated observation standards, grading norms, conduct of visits, and the like may be dictated by an administrator to adjunct faculty. They can accept or reject conditions of employment, but once accepted, supervisory staff are usually content to do the job expected, rather than examine the procedures and seek points of continuity or discontinuity with their tenets of practice.

On the other hand, tenure-track faculty have faculty meetings, teacher education councils, and other formal and informal forums for discussing changes, innovations, and problems. Additionally, the tenure-track faculty are more stable in terms of job longevity. They are more likely to remain in a position long enough to see that needed changes are made. They hold deep convictions regarding education, learning, and teaching, and their reputation in part rests on the excellence of the program in which they function.

As a supervisor of student teachers, the university faculty is in a unique position to evaluate the teacher education program as it relates to student teaching. As an insider, the professor is aware of the goals of the program and how the various elements of the program should function, of how the student teacher should perform. The professor, as a fully functioning faculty member in the department responsible for the program, knows the procedures to effect change and can take the necessary action to shore up weak program elements.

A major benefit to the higher education institution of having a university professor supervising student teachers is the personal contact with K-12 faculty. The university professor serves as a public relations representative to the schools. A professor supervising student teachers makes invaluable contacts for future development projects, grant sites, and research locations. University professors, as student teaching supervisors, are in a position to recruit for graduate programs. Most K-12 teachers are bound by monetary and family responsibilities to graduate programs offered by local higher education institutions.

Where competing programs exist, it is often the personal contact with professors that is the deciding factor on a choice of institution. Thus, particularly in impersonal large institutions, personal knowledge of a professor who has been in your classroom, with whom you have collaborated in grooming a student teacher, operates as a public relations benefit in recruiting graduate students. That the graduate program is a quality one is assumed.

Additionally, professors observing in schools receive first-hand information about the reality of K-12 school life. The professor's theoretical concerns are tested in the school arena, perhaps to be confirmed, modified, or even abandoned. Professors also garner vignettes of teachers, problems and solutions in dealing with learners. These vignettes then enrich the professor's own courses at the university, bringing real and current concerns about teaching into preservice education. Coordinating teachers often report their student teachers are "teacher pleasers." It is difficult to convince the student teacher to attempt something different from what the teacher does. The coordinating teacher often accepts a student teacher to have contact with curricular innovations. When a university professor, particularly one who may have taught a student teacher, supervises, the student teacher may be more likely to model what is taught at the university rather than attempt "teacher pleasing" safe behavior.

A final benefit of a professor as the student teaching supervisor is that the professor, often more secure by tenure than adjunct supervisors, will offer continuity in the sense of advice to former student teachers as they continue into their first years of teaching.

In some student teaching experiences, students observe the cooperating teacher in acts that were not advocated in the student's university courses. When a university professor is well known for one stance on a particular educational issue, that stance is known by the student teacher; but if the cooperating teacher does not embrace the professor's position, conflict may result, with the student teacher in the middle. One way of resolving this dilemma is to take the position that the student and the university representative are in the schools on sufferance and are obligated to act as guests. The student should, therefore, conform to the cooperating teacher's position. The student is admonished to do the "right" thing in the safety of his or her own classroom. This is a congenial solution to the problem. It serves, however, to separate and fragment the education program into theory versus practice, with no dialogue between the two parties. When the conflict between university and school practice is clearly a case of malpractice, the university supervisor must always intercede on the side of safe practice.

In the practice of collegiality, rather than congeniality, both university and field are involved in discussion concerning the entire teaching and learning process. Field cooperating teachers are not part of one program fragment, but are a cohesive voice in a continuing dialogue among equal professionals.

Possible conflicts over philosophy, practice, curriculum, or other facets of the teaching process are resolved to mutual satisfaction. Both parties adapt to the requirements of the situation, always keeping the learner's best interests in the forefront of the discussion.

After detailing the program benefits of a professor engaging in direct student teaching supervision, the department chair must also weigh the debits in such faculty assignments. The university system does not reward such supervision. Student teaching supervision is labor- and time-intensive. Although national professional guidelines establish 1:18 as the supervisor to student teaching ratio, even this limit can be overwhelming. This is especially true in regional programs where student teachers may be placed in widely spaced schools, inevitably requiring extensive travel.

The chair of a department responsible for a teacher education program must view student teaching as an essential organ of the total teacher education enterprise and maintain close contact with it. To maintain the vitality and health of the total teacher education program, the department chair cannot abdicate responsibilities for supervision, for evaluation, for developing sources, or for links to graduate programs. Even when, as is often the case, there is present a full-time field coordinator with a staff of student teaching supervisors, the chair must see that student teaching remains firmly within the total program and that it serves to weave and braid both theory and practice into a tapestry of successful teaching and learning.

References

Bolin, F. S. (1990). Helping student teachers think about teaching: Another look at law. *Journal of Teacher Education, 41*(1), 10-19.

Bransford, J. D., Vye, N. J., Adams, L. T., & Perfetta, G. A. (1989). Learning skills and the acquisition of knowledge. In A. Lesgold & R. Glaser (Eds.), *Foundations for a psychology of education* (pp. 199-249). Hillsdale, NJ: Erlbaum.

Coates, T. J., & Thorenson, C. E. (1976). Teacher anxiety: A review with recommendations. *Review of Educational Research, 46,* 159-184.

Evans, E. E., & Tribble, M. (1986). Perceived teaching problems, self-efficacy, and commitment to teaching. *Journal of Educational Research, 80*(2), 81-85.

Goodlad, J. I., Soder, R., & Sirotnik, K. A. (Eds.). (1990). *Places where teachers are taught.* San Francisco: Jossey-Bass.

Hoy, W. K., & Woolfolk, A. E. (1990). Prospective teachers' sense of efficacy and beliefs about control. *Journal of Experimental Psychology, 82*(1), 81-91.

Katz, L., & Raths, J. D. (1982). The best of intentions for the education of teachers. *Action in Teacher Education, 4,* 8-16.

Kazelskis, R., Reeves-Kazelskis, C., & Kersh, M. E. (1991). *Effects of student teaching on teaching concerns and efficacy.* Paper presented at the annual meeting of the Mid-South Educational Research Association, Lexington, KY.

Kazelskis, R., Reeves-Kazelskis, C., & Kersh, M. E. (1993). Work environment preference. *The Professional Educator, 16*(1), 13-19.

Mississippi Teacher and Administrator Education, Certification, and Development. (1990). Jackson: Bureau of School Improvement, State Department of Education.

Scheffler, A. J., Richmond, M. G., Kersh, M. E., & Dana, M. E. (1991). Paper presented at the Third International Conference on Assessing Quality in Higher Education, Bath, England.

Veenman, S. (1984). Perceived problems of beginning teachers. *Review of Educational Research, 54*, 143-178.

Recommended Reading

Diez, M. E., Richardson, V., & Pearson, P. D. (1994). *Setting standards and educating teachers. A national conversation.* Washington, DC: American Association of Colleges for Teacher Education.

Jones, D. R. (1982). The influence of length and level of student teaching on pupil control ideology. *High School Journal, 66,* 220-225.

Kazelskis, R., Kersh, M. E., & Reeves, C. K. (1989). *Undergraduate teacher education preparation and level of concern about teaching.* Paper presented at the annual meeting of the Mid-South Educational Research Association, Little Rock, AR.

Knowles, J. G., & Cole, A. L. (1994). *Through preservice teachers' eyes.* New York: Macmillan.

Pigge, F. L., & Marso, R. N. (1990). A longitudinal assessment of the affective impact of preservice training on prospective teachers. *Journal of Experimental Education,* 283-389.

Roberts, R. A., & Blankenship, J. W. (1970). The relationship between the change in pupil control ideology of student teachers and the student teachers' pupil control ideology. *Journal of Research in Science Teaching, 7,* 315-320.

Roe, B. D., & Ross, E. P. (1994). *Student teaching and field experiences handbook.* New York: Macmillan.

❖ 10 ❖

Bits and Pieces

Everything Else You Wanted to Know About Designing and Implementing Field Experience Programs

KENNETH BURRETT
GLORIA APPELT SLICK

Imagine! Imagine a field experience program your way. The authors of Book I have shared many provocative ideas, perspectives, and accomplishments. We hope that this information will be useful in supporting and encouraging the creation of successful programs for new teachers.

Imagination

Often the limit on building a successful field program is the inability to imagine possibilities. To restate this proposition, the vision of a quality program is informed by the creativity, analytical ability, information resources, and, ultimately, the capacity of the program leadership to bring forth a vision of a quality program. Many argue that developing vision is the most important element in developing organizations that deliver quality services (Collins & Porras, 1991). Proponents for the application of leadership theory in educational settings reflect that there must be a vision that is inspired by a leader, and that the leader must be pragmatic (Weller, 1994). The vision inspires program quality and serves as the overarching organizational construct for a program.

The vision or plan precedes action. Plan, then do. In the business of leading and managing field programs, ideas are judged best as they are evaluated in practice. The field director must be a person of action. The press of daily requirements often impacts the ability to stay with a plan. Nevertheless, our authors provide examples of vision and doing.

Developing Vision

The goal of the field director is to develop a shared vision of a quality teacher education program that is owned by the teacher education unit and is specifically reflected in field based programs. Planning and consensus building are clearly necessary characteristics of building a vision. Vision statements typically include the following:

- Identify core values and beliefs
- Identify an ideal, as differentiated from pragmatic compromises

What bits of inspiration about our core beliefs and values have our authors brought forth? Think!

- Educational excellence requires unique partnerships.
- Involvement of practitioners in program delivery adds vitality and creativity.

- Unique partnership arrangements energize teacher education.
- The efficacy of field-based programs is related to organizational variables.
- There are effective ways of motivating professors, classroom teachers, and students. And above all,
- Program creation requires individual initiative and team building.

Program Process: Bureaucratic or Collegial

The chapters in this book form a rich database of conceptual issues and process considerations. Review of these works yields some bits and pieces that can be important in designing programs. Program developers might consider:

- Reflection on the impact of the social context in shaping teacher education programs.
- Implications of Total Quality Management leadership theory on the process of structuring programs.
- Assumptions about individual motivation and the impact of group interaction, especially the propositions of Theory Z.
- Performance standards, as proposed in NCATE, NASDEC, and INTASC documents.
- Innovative models of design and assessment. And above all,
- Opportunities for connecting the substance and form of field-based programs with the curriculum of the teacher education unit.

Our authors indicate that creating successful programs requires designing a system that harnesses the energy of faculty, practitioners, researchers, and visionaries to develop cutting-edge paradigms for teacher education. Such a mandate might well recognize the following assumptions:

- Leadership is not confined to those holding status positions in the power echelon.
- Good human relations are essential to group production.
- Responsibility as well as power can be shared.
- Those affected by the program should share in decision making.
- The individual finds security in shared decision making.
- Unity of purpose is secured through consensus and group loyalty.
- Maximum production is obtained in a threat-free climate.
- Line staff organizations should be used exclusively for dividing labor and implementation.
- Regulations and procedures recognize that the need for authority arises from the situation. (Morphet, Johns, & Reller, 1982, pp. 77-79)

The process used in designing the program ideally allows for stakeholders' ownership. The assumptions that undergird the program support substantially different interactive processes and, consequently, different program accomplishments. There is reason to encourage the empowerment of program participants. The vision includes consideration of the interactive process.

Program Organization: The Team

Who is responsible for making the field program work? The answer includes a broad constituency. The director of the field experience program is responsible for functioning as a very influential member of a leadership team and certainly maintains responsibility for such administrative details as contracts, placement correspondence, registration of students, verifying medical records, and ascertaining eligibility of potential students, among other general management responsibilities.

However, the emerging trend is one of shared responsibility. Program leadership is often a mutual responsibility, including faculty and administrators from the teacher education unit as a whole as well as members from local schools and districts.

Innovative programs at the college or university level connect academic and on-site experiences for enhanced learning. Running courses on block scheduling is not an unusual practice. The current thrust, reflected both in the literature and in accrediting standards, is to include classroom observation and participation as an essential part of university-based class work. Such practices enhance learning and facilitate the ability of teacher education students to translate theory into practice. As such, the curricula are inextricably linked.

In current practice, the definition of just who composes the faculty of teacher education programs is undergoing redefinition. Increasingly, classroom teachers, instructional team leaders, head teachers, supervisors, principals, and other members of basic education are assuming roles as full and equal members of the teacher educating team. This often includes responsibilities that range from placing student teachers in buildings or districts, establishing mentor and apprentice relationships, and serving in an adjunct capacity with the participating college or university, to actively participating in assessment and evaluation.

In this emerging organizational paradigm, the construct of team is replacing the top-down structure. The field director is becoming more of a coach and less of a boss. In designing a communication and management structure, the field director might consider:

- Decentralizing decision making
- Establishing a system of quality circles with defined tasks
- Forming councils to connect field programs with teacher education programs
- Giving school-based practitioners status and recognition as legitimate members of the teacher education team
- Establishing an advisory group to handle issues of both policy and management
- Considering arrangements that involve practitioners in course or module instruction

- Negotiating opportunities for university and college faculty to be involved in schools
- Developing contract arrangements with local educational agencies that specify roles and responsibilities

Now is the time to recognize the cooperative potential in teacher education. The new team concept includes members from a broader constituency within the university, as well as experts from the practicing profession in our public and private schools. The opportunity and the challenge lie ahead.

Assessment

Imagination certainly includes dreams of creative possibilities, plans to allow for empowering moments and reflective opportunities, and prospects for redefined structures. Imagination certainly leads to new directions. Although responsibilities of leadership include knowing where and how to proceed, it is also incumbent on leaders to know whether the destination has been reached.

The best of programs require the best of assessments. It is important to assess the program itself as well as the outcomes of the teacher education candidates themselves.

For the program, assessment is an important mechanism for monitoring and adjusting. With appropriate feedback, the field director as coach can monitor and adjust the team process as necessary. Often feedback becomes information that can improve program quality. Assessment is a mechanism for involving all participants in meaningful decision making.

Assessment is integral to the instructional process housed in field programs. The criterion for success in teacher education programs is the successful outcomes of the participants, their performances. These outcomes are cognitive and affective in nature and include attitudes, ideals, instructional design abilities, teaching behaviors, and the ability to implement varying teaching strategies and models. The available data are extensive and diverse. Assessment approaches must be correspondingly complex. Field directors might consider:

- Designing an assessment and evaluation model
- Developing portfolio formats
- Designing formative evaluation into program development
- Developing portfolios to promote student growth
- Identifying criteria for acceptable portfolio entries
- Developing structures for evaluating portfolios
- Deciding the important perspectives to document, and
- Developing a mechanism for modifying program design based on analysis of student outcomes and program evaluation

Creating Successful Programs

The successful program results both from hard work and from inspiration. The field director, as coach, is responsible for identifying the essential ingredients that contribute to outstanding programs. Furthermore, responsibility includes defining and redefining the teacher education team. Inspirational leadership is necessary. Successful programs require leadership, and they are also characterized by sound organizational management. Knowledge of traditional and nontraditional learning modes is evident. Given the above, an occasional creative moment can spark the creation of a successful program.

The advice for the aspiring field director is evident: Become an excellent manager and an excellent leader. All the examples of cutting-edge programs evidence attention to organizational detail. The difference that makes outstanding programs, though, is attributable to insight, knowledge, and imagination.

References

Collins, J. C., & Porras, J. T. (1991, Fall). Organization vision and visioning organizations. *California Management Review*, 30-52.

Morphet, E. L., Johns, R. L., & Reller, T. L. (1982). *Education organization and administrations: Concepts, practices, and issues* (4th ed.). Englewood Cliffs, NJ: Prentice Hall.

Weller, D. (1994). *TQM leadership.* Paper presented at ATE conference, Snowbird, UT.

Recommended Reading

Interstate New Teacher Assessment and Support Consortium. (1992). *Model standards for beginning teacher licensing and development: A resource for state dialogue* (pp. 10-30).

National Association of State Directors of Teacher Education and Certification (NASDEC). (1993). *Outcome-based standards and portfolio assessment: Outcome-based teacher education standards for the elementary, middle, and high school levels* (2nd ed.).

Index

CORWIN
PRESS

The Corwin Press Logo—a raven striding across an open book— represents the happy union of courage and learning. We are a professional-level publisher of books and journals for K-12 educators, and we are committed to creating and providing resources that embody these qualities. Corwin's motto is "Success for All Learners."